"At last a commonsense and business-oriented approach ↑ book gives very practical instruction that is easy to apply. for it."
—*Nancy K. M. Rees, Vice President and Chief*

"This is a short, concise volume that gets right to the hea~~rt of process impro~~ with specific, concrete steps and excellent examples. It's a book you can use today."
—*Dennis J. Frailey, Principal Fellow, Raytheon Company*

"If your customers demand better, faster cycle times and higher quality products, your software development and project management process must change. *Making Process Improvement Work* shows you how to define your real goals and devise practical strategies for achieving them. Of course, if you're perfectly happy with the way your development teams perform and your customers are always thrilled with your products, don't read this book."
—*From the Foreword by Karl Wiegers, Principal Consultant, Process Impact*

"As a manager of a software development organization, I found the book interesting, meaningful, and useful. In my work at Bradley Company, I've used the goal-problem approach that the book advocates and have firsthand knowledge that it works well. We've made remarkable progress with it. I specifically liked the following about the book:

- It is short and concise, which is refreshing. Nothing is more irritating than reading through a bunch of fluff. When that happens, I go into skim reading mode and possibly miss important points or the book isn't finished.
- The examples are very good, especially rewording of problems into goals and the compelling versus noncompelling goal examples. The how-to's are very good. I'm using some today. After reading this book, I plan to start using the risk management approach, especially the prioritization technique.
- Insights into different companies given in the examples are great for learning. Very few people in the industry have the background to credibly write a book containing this valuable information.
- The book answered my questions, such as 'How do you vary the approach based on the size of an organization and what happens when you want to achieve a CMM certification and there are residual practices that don't match a business problem?'"
—*Teresa M. Light, Senior Vice President and General Manager, Bradley Company*

"This book delivers a very clear message about what the focus of the improvement process should be. It makes one stop and think on what the objective really is. Do I want to get certified on whatever the trend the last consultant brought in or do I want to achieve a determined business goal? People will have to take two steps back and re-think about their goals.

The book is very easy to read. It does not throw the reader off with high technical jargon. I have the responsibility to oversee all software projects at the largest insurance company in Guatemala, but I would even give it to an end user or somebody from a nontechnical department with the purpose to acquire buy-in in the improvement process."
—*Alejandro Acevedo, Seguros G&T (Guatemala)*

"At IBM, I was for many years, a key member of the OS/390 project office, working directly with development managers to assure their deliverables met lifecycle development standards of all kinds. Since leaving IBM, I have worked as a consultant in similar roles. Guidance and tips in this book have helped me land a very good assignment as a 'software process improvement mentor' in a large insurance company.

The book is unique; much of what is written can be found in a variety of sources but not in one book."

—*Wayne Yaddow, Consultant*

"I would buy the book, because it is straightforward, with real-life examples and to the point (in Dutch 'gezond verstand' translated directly 'healthy mind, brains')."

—*Maurits Van Cappellen, Alcatel (Belgium)*

"This book is a blessing in disguise! It is well written, has examples and templates that can be easily used—a great start point for many. It covers all the highlights from management support to culture. I also really like how the book works the problem set and identification of goals into positive, desired state nomenclature. By doing so it can actually propel folks into action. The language of the book is written so that even beginners in the SPI world can get immediate understanding of how to start/continue."

—*Barbara Marasco, Xerox*

"I found this book exceedingly practical and helpful, particularly in planning an improvement program. I was able to use its advice on planning with no further research or guidance and was very pleased with the results.

I expect to refer to these ideas repeatedly and to recommend this book to others who do process improvement. The real-world examples and step-by-step approach are very effective at making the reader feel capable of tackling an improvement program and succeeding at it. Finally, but actually uppermost in my mind, I fully subscribe to the philosophy of the authors that we should undertake improvements because they will help our business."

—*Kathy Rhode, USA*

"Bravo! A book that provides real help with the 'critical' issues in a process improvement program. The risk management process is very 'doable' and the discussion of the adoption and resistance issues is exactly what people on the process improvement journey need to know. The approach is extremely practical. I especially applaud the 'don't force it' attitude with advice like 'If there are no unmet needs, goals, or problems to solve, then you should mutually agree that nothing will be done.'"

—*Helen Smelser, Texas Instruments, Dallas*

"The numerous examples, cases, graphs, and templates give the reader the tools to start the improvements in his or her own organization. Furthermore, the book is fun and easy to read."

—*Robbert Schravendijk, Quint Wellington Redwood (The Netherlands)*

"This is a great book. It is evident it is written from real experience. The chapter summaries are awesome. Anyone starting out or progressing in an improvement project will find this book extremely helpful. The content covers the important steps in action planning. It remains generic rather than tackling the specific practices of one of the accepted models. [The] illustrations are excellent. More than are usually presented in a small handbook. The expertise of the authors and the Process Group is unquestioned. This work further demonstrates their competence in leading improvement efforts and the ability to relate to the managers and change agents."

—*Al Bennett, Software Engineering Manager, ITT Industries, Aerospace/Communications Division*

"I like the approach described in the book and only regret that we did not have this insight two years ago when we first started our software process improvement journey. We could have avoided many of the pitfalls."

—*Tom Tougas, Harmon Industries, MO*

MAKING
PROCESS
IMPROVEMENT
WORK

MAKING
PROCESS
IMPROVEMENT
WORK

A Concise Action Guide for Software
Managers and Practitioners

Neil S. Potter
Mary E. Sakry

✦✦Addison-Wesley

Boston • San Francisco • New York • Toronto • Montreal
London • Munich • Paris • Madrid
Capetown • Sydney • Tokyo • Singapore • Mexico City

The publisher offers discounts on this book when ordered in quantity for special sales. For more information, please contact:

Pearson Education Corporate Sales Division
One Lake Street
Upper Saddle River, NJ 07458
(800) 382-3419
corpsales@pearsontechgroup.com

Visit AW on the Web: www.awl.com/cseng/

Library of Congress Control Number: 2002101208

ISBN 0-201-77577-8
Text printed on recycled paper
1 2 3 4 5 6 7 8 9 10—MA—0605040302
First printing, March 2002

Contents

Foreword

I have never met a software developer who can honestly state, "I am building software today as well as software could ever be built." Therefore, I expect many people to be interested in Neil Potter and Mary Sakry's *Making Process Improvement Work*. Magazine articles on software process improvement abound, and several books are already available on specific process models, including the Capability Maturity Model for Software, SPICE, and ISO9001. Mary and Neil now help close a significant gap in the literature: the gap between model and practice, between concept and application.

Although many software organizations have reaped benefits from sustained improvement initiatives, others struggle to make headway. Too many organizations develop a checklist mentality targeted at achieving the next process maturity level or passing an audit. Not only does this strategy often fail to address the real problems, but process development for its own sake leaves a bad taste in the team members' mouths. Neil and Mary remind us to focus on pragmatic mechanisms for achieving superior business results, drawing from both established process models and the entire set of software engineering practices. They don't offer a simple silver-bullet prescription to solve all of your development and quality problems. Instead, they present numerous guiding principles and a process improvement strategy that any software organization can apply to meet ever-more-challenging demands.

This book provides solid advice about the most sensible approach to improving any organization's performance: Define your goals, identify the barriers that prevent you from achieving them, and implement focused changes to remove those barriers. Neil and Mary speak to software development managers and people who are responsible for leading an improvement initiative to a successful outcome. They encourage us to link our process improvement actions with our organization's desired business goals. They define a systematic approach to planning, implementing, and assessing the results of an improvement program. This book collects lessons learned from The Process Group's many years of hands-on process improvement experience.

If your customers demand better, faster cycle times and higher quality products, your software development and project management processes must change. *Making Process Improvement Work* shows you how to define your real goals and devise practical strategies for achieving them. Of course, if you're perfectly happy with the way your development teams perform and your customers are always thrilled with your products, don't read this book.

Karl Wiegers, principal consultant at Process Impact
Author of Creating a Software Engineering Culture,
Dorset House Publishing, 1996; Software Requirements,
Microsoft Press, 1999; and Peer Reviews in Software:
A Practical Guide, *Addison-Wesley, 2001*

Preface

WHO SHOULD READ THIS BOOK

You are probably more than aware of the problems facing your software development organization. The list of problems usually starts with an overwhelming string of commitments and optimistic deadlines. For example, the marketing department has been promised that the product will be shipped by the end of the year. Customers have been told that everything will be delivered on time, and top management has established year-end bonuses based on meeting these dates. Now the programmers are working progressively longer hours, and the system test group is anxiously awaiting the software to begin intensive testing. The technical writers are lost in 300 pull-down menus and cannot get feedback from the programmers. Meanwhile, support engineers are still fixing defects from the previous release and are not optimistic that their lives will improve any time soon.

On top of all this, your group has been signed up to use the new standards and processes developed by corporate engineering. At best, this sounds like just another documentation exercise with little or no positive impact on your group. You have been through numerous improvement programs, each one consuming time, but not providing you with the gains for which you had hoped. The benefits you did see were quickly forgotten in subsequent projects.

Sound familiar? If you have lived in an organization like this for a year or two, you are probably a little tired of the chronic problems, new improvement schemes, and lack of real progress. If you are ready for a straightforward, systematic approach to improvement, read on.

This book is for managers and practitioners. If you are the director of a division, read the book to understand how your group can systematically improve and tie those improvements directly to your business goals. If you are a project or program manager tasked with developing a specific product, use the information to plan, deploy, and track improvements within your team. If you are a process improvement, quality management, or development engineer, apply the techniques in each chapter to coach your team through its improvement journey.

HOW THIS BOOK IS ORGANIZED

Throughout this book we guide you in achieving better organizational results. You will understand the critical steps needed to implement lasting and worthwhile change. The book will stimulate your thinking about

- ◆ How software development organizations improve
- ◆ What they improve
- ◆ How they deploy and track improvements

Making Process Improvement Work is based on our work with more than 3,000 software professionals representing some 100 companies around the world. We have included stories and examples from individuals in these companies who are using our ideas as they travel on their road to improvement. We have seen what works and what does not.

The book is small and concise so that you can quickly absorb and use the information. It is organized into three chapters using the concepts of the Shewhart cycle for planning and managing improvement [Deming86].

Developing a Plan

In Chapter 1 you will develop an improvement action plan based on the business goals and problems of your organization. This approach addresses the frustration that many people experience when improvement programs do not relate to the project work being done. In this chapter you'll learn about

- Setting compelling goals for your improvement program
- Directing all improvement towards achieving business goals and solving the organization's problems
- Developing an action plan based on the defined goals and problems
- Using an improvement model or standard to address the goals and problems
- Deriving metrics for the goals
- Identifying potential future problems (risks) with the action plan and mitigating the highest priority risks

Implementing the Plan

Chapter 2 describes techniques for deploying new practices across the organization. These techniques address the problems of resistance, unwieldy solutions, and slow deployment. The central themes in this chapter are

- Applying selling strategies to deploy new practices
- Increasing the speed of deployment by working with the willing and the needy first

♦ Reducing the risk of failure by building and deploying solutions in increments

♦ Delaying policy document creation and edicts until each solution has been practiced and is well tested

♦ Using existing resources to increase the speed of deployment

Checking Progress

Chapter 3 presents techniques for checking the progress of your improvement program and taking corrective actions based on what you learn. Checking progress is an essential activity to provide the organization with feedback when pursuing business goals and solving problems. The resulting data allows for early problem detection, early correction, and improved visibility to management on improvement progress. In this chapter you'll explore methods for

♦ Using metrics to track progress based on defined goals

♦ Determining corrective actions needed to get the improvement program back on track

♦ Clarifying lessons learned and actions needed to make future executions of the improvement cycle more effective

As you read the book, you will be referred to the appendices that provide additional details for the examples given in each of the chapters.

Appendices A and B are examples referenced in Chapter 1 where practices in the CMM and CMMI frameworks are mapped to business goals and project problems. Appendix C contains a full example of an improvement action plan. Appendix D expands upon the risk management plan example started in Chapter 1. Appendix E summarizes the two maturity models used in the book, that is, the CMM (1.1) and CMMI (1.1). Appendix F provides a complete definition of the mini-assessment process described in Chapter 3, a technique used to track improvement progress.

Using Improvement Models and Standards

Several improvement models and standards exist that can save you much time, such as the Software Engineering Institute (SEI) Capability Maturity Model (CMM) and Capability Maturity Model Integration (CMMI),[1] SPICE, BOOTSTRAP, and ISO9001.[2] In each of the chapters we reference a model or standard as a *framework*. These documents incorporate lessons learned from numerous people worldwide who have studied and implemented improvement. If you use them wisely, you can significantly improve your success rate. If you use them academically, you can waste much time. In this book, we show how to integrate these resources with your improvement program.

The examples in the book include the SEI CMM and CMMI frameworks. If you are using another model or standard, such as SPICE, BOOTSTRAP, or ISO9001, substitute it where we refer to the CMM. If you are not using any model or standard, the techniques described in the book will help you develop your own improvement actions to address your organization's issues.

---

1. See Appendix E for summaries of the SEI, CMM v1.1, and CMMI v1.1.
2. See [Zahran98] for summaries of SPICE, BOOTSTRAP, and ISO9001.

Acknowledgments

A number of people took the time to review the manuscript and offer recommendations for improvement; they have our deep gratitude. Special thanks go to Terry Light, Randy Reetz, Peggy Koontz, and Phil Foell for many of the examples used in the book. Kathleen Rhode, Robert Funicello, Mark Paulk, Karen Skinner, Norman Hammock, Ed Weller, Doris Sturzenberger, Elaine Anselm, Phyllis Moore, Karl Wiegers, Bonnie Reuscher, Linda Westfall, Helen Smelser, William Burns, Michael Reed, Terry Sardina, Cathy Henderson, Christian Bund, Alejandro Acevedo, George Yamamura, Robbert Schravendijk, Barbara Marasco, Peter Hantos, Blaine Couveau, Libby Dunn, and Peggy Fouts commented on various versions of the manuscript—a time-consuming undertaking for which we are sincerely grateful.

Thanks also to Carolyn Rodda Lincoln, Carol Robinson, Vanessa Lee Otto, Jim Hudec, Pat Gough, Tommaso Landi, Henrietta Foster, Mark Reinhart, Kimberly Brown, Tom Keuten, J. Jentink, Tom Tougas, Wayne Yaddow, James Heires, Bill Dreher, and Bowen Ormsby for their numerous comments and suggestions.

Of course, there would be no book without the faith of Peter Gordon from Addison-Wesley, who gave us the opportunity to publish this work.

1

Developing a Plan

"Unplanned process improvement is wishful thinking."
—Watts Humphrey, *Managing the Software Process*
[Humphrey89]

There are many approaches to improvement that we have seen during the last 14 years. Two stand out as the most common. With the first approach, small teams document the tasks they typically perform when they develop software. The notion is that if their current practices are documented, they can be shared among the development group and the best ones will become "best practices." When everyone adopts these best practices, the theory goes, then the quality problem will be solved. Unfortunately, the result is often a stack of paper that is ignored.

With the second approach, a company strides toward the achievement of an improvement framework such as ISO9001 or the Software Engineering Institute Capability Maturity Model (SEI CMM). This journey takes place in response to a goal stating something like, "Achieve CMM Level 3 by December." The primary focus typically consists of forming teams organized around the framework and creating procedures that describe how the company should operate. Because the framework requires that procedures must exist, documenting them appears to be a logical first step and the most direct path to the goal. The decision to adopt an improvement framework is sound, and when used appropriately, leads to significant improvements. Unfortunately, the result is often a mixture of some benefits, universal frustration, and lots of paper.

In these two examples, the approach to improvement is the problem, not the use of a framework or the definition of best practices. These "process-centric" approaches can lead to real gains. However, they have a high risk of failure because they encourage teams to focus on a target (for example, process documentation) that is all too often seen as irrelevant to the real work of the organization. Success depends on each document author's ability to communicate the rationale behind his recommended process and how it applies to current and future project work. When this communication breaks down, the rest of the organization often perceives the process-centric approach as *yet another pointless quality program.*

The white line in Figure 1–1 illustrates a common result of the process-centric approach. The line starts, wanders around, and results in a group of frustrated people disappointed with their gains. At this point, the developers look up at the mountaintop (in other words, their product delivery goal), stop activity on the process improvement program, and start coding the product.

When an improvement program is focused on a process framework, it is common for it to be treated as nonessential—a luxury that is only affordable when the business climate is rosy. Even when the business climate blossoms, we are too busy to fit in additional activities, and again, improvement is seen as an unnecessary task.

An alternative approach is to focus on the organization's goals and problems, and to tie improvement activities directly

Starting point

Common result:
Lost in the trees

Figure 1–1   The process-centric approach to improvement.

to current project work. With this approach, improvement focuses on the real issues of the organization, with each change driven by a specific need. The scope of the improvement program is not defined by an improvement framework, but rather by the organization's goals and problems.

The goal-problem approach described in this book keeps the organization focused on compelling issues that people want to fix now. The improvement plan centers on the organization's challenges, with small actions continuously taken to move the organization toward its goals. Improvement frameworks are adopted fully but in small pieces, with each piece fitted to a project problem or goal. Improvement progress is measured by improved organizational results. Figure 1–2 illustrates the goal-problem approach for planning an improvement program.

Scope the Improvement

- Establish plan ownership.
- State the major goals and problems.
- Group the problems related to each goal.
- Ensure that the goals and problems are crystal clear and compelling.
- Set goal priorities.
- Derive metrics for the goals.

Develop an Action Plan

- Enumerate actions using brainstorming and a process framework.
- Organize the action plan based on the goals and problems.
- Add placeholders for checking progress and taking corrective action.

Determine Risks and Plan to Mitigate

- Determine the scope of the risk session.
- Select the team and moderator.
- Identify risks.
- Analyze risks.
- Plan to mitigate.
- Plan for periodic risk review.

Figure 1–2   The goal-problem approach for planning an improvement program.

SCOPE THE IMPROVEMENT

Figure 1–3 highlights one goal of the organization. This goal may be the delivery of a product, the completion of a software installation, or the upgrade of a database. The goal could also be to meet deadlines 100 percent of the time or to reduce rework to 25 percent of the total development effort. These are business goals [Hill79]. The goal-problem approach starts with business goals and uncovers problems that prevent the achievement of each goal [Sakry01].

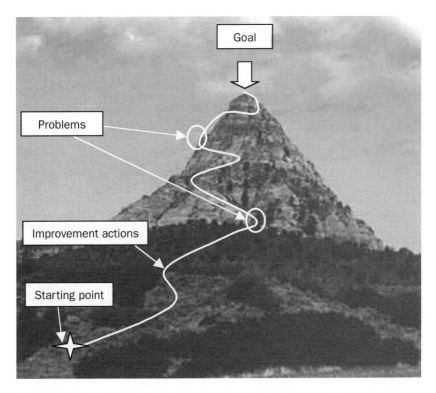

Figure 1–3 The goal-problem approach to improvement.

An improvement action plan is then constructed to address these problems and to move the organization toward its goals [Robbins98].

To scope the improvement effort, follow these steps:

1. Establish plan ownership.
2. State the major goals and problems.
3. Group the problems related to each goal.
4. Ensure that the goals and problems are crystal clear and compelling.
5. Set goal priorities.
6. Derive metrics for the goals.

Step 1: Establish Plan Ownership

The improvement plan you create will need an owner. Identify this person now to ensure that the owner's needs are met by the plan. If you wait until your plan is complete, you face the risk of no one wanting the plan. The plan owner should be the same person who owns the business goals being addressed by the plan. For most business goals, a project manager, program manager, senior manager, or division head are likely candidates. Don't invest too much time in planning your improvement effort until you find someone who wants the plan.

As you develop the plan following the steps defined in this chapter, it is likely that you will appoint different individuals to be responsible for each section of the plan, in addition to the primary owner of the whole plan. For example, the marketing person will want to own the section related to making sound commitments to the customer. Similarly, the test manager will want to own the section on improving product testing, and the development manager will want to own the section that addresses project planning and product design. Motivation to own a plan section comes from an individual's desire to see her issues addressed by the plan.

The primary owner of the improvement plan should not be the software engineering process group, the software quality assurance (SQA) group, or similar support function. Support functions can share ownership and responsibility for the plan with the owner of the business goals, but they cannot be held solely accountable for accomplishing these goals. Typically, support functions are charged with providing tangible and useful support to the software development teams during plan execution.

Step 2: State the Major Goals and Problems

During one client visit to help plan an improvement program, we learned that the group had initially scoped its improvement effort to the six key process areas of Level 2 in the CMM.[1] We suggested that the developers and managers temporarily forget about Level 2 and state all the major goals they were trying to achieve during the next 6 to 18 months. We then asked them to state their problems related to software development. After one hour of discussion, they created the two lists in Figure 1–4:

The idea of temporarily forgetting process-related goals (such as CMM Level 2 or ISO9001) is very difficult for some organizations to accept. Goals such as these have been drummed into many people so intensely that temporarily shelving them can sound like a major change in strategy and direction. It is critical that the target of the improvement program be relevant to the organization's needs. You accomplish this by first identifying the organization's needs and then aligning the improvement program (including the use of improvement frameworks) with those needs. If your current improvement program is not clearly connected to the needs of the organization, it may be wasting many valuable resources.

When you create a list of goals and problems, inviting the stakeholders to the session is essential for creating buy-in. Stakeholders are all the people who will be affected by the plan. For example, the stakeholders for a division would be the division head, his or her direct reports, and key opinion leaders within the group. The stakeholders for a single project would be the team members and their manager.

If you are working with a senior manager to establish goals and problems, don't assume that you have to approach this

---

1. For SEI CMM (v1.1), the six key process areas of Level 2 are Requirements Management, Software Project Planning, Software Project Tracking and Oversight, Software Configuration Management, Software Quality Assurance, and Software Subcontract Management. See Appendix E for further CMM references and definitions.

Goals

1. Create predictable schedules.
2. Successfully deliver product X.
3. Reduce rework.
4. Improve the performance of our core software product.
5. Keep customers happy.
6. Keep making a profit.

Problems

1. Need better requirements. Requirements tracking not in place. Changes to requirements are not tracked; code does not match specification at test time.
2. Management direction unclear for product version 2.3. Goals change often.
3. Quality department does not have training in product and test skills.
4. Unclear status of software changes.
5. Lack of resources and skills allocated to software design.
6. Changes to specifications and documentation are not communicated effectively to documentation and test groups.
7. Finding time to do critical activities (product development) is difficult. Time is spent on crisis activities.
8. Test plan does not necessarily encompass things that matter to the customer.
9. Defect repairs break essential product features.
10. Wrong files (for example, dynamic link libraries) are put on CD. Unsure of the correct ones.
11. Revising the project plan is difficult. Items drop off, new things are added, plan is out of date.
12. We don't understand our capacity and do not have one list of all the work we have to do.
13. Schedule tracking and communication of changes to affected groups is poor.
14. Testers do not have tools to manage their test activities.
15. Customers are unhappy. There are approximately 300 outstanding defects that have not been addressed.

Figure 1–4   The goals and problems of one organization.

person any differently than anyone else. Senior managers have goals and problems too. In fact, they will appreciate your direct questions regarding the issues that bother them. Ask them what project or business goals they have for the next 6 to 18 months, and what problems cause their organization the most difficulty. Listen to their response, take careful notes, and at the end of the session, test your understanding of what they said.

When you have created the initial list of problems and goals, consider expanding the stakeholder roster if issues on the list affect other areas of the organization. In the previous two lists in Figure 1–4, the improvement team added the marketing manager as a stakeholder after noting the problem *Management direction unclear for product version 2.3* on their list. (Throughout the book we often refer to the stakeholders as your customers.)

Step 3: Group the Problems Related to Each Goal

A long list of problems and goals resulting from step 2 can be overwhelming. You can simplify the list by grouping the problems that prevent each goal from being achieved. In the following example (Table 1–1), grouping problems and goals reduced the list from 21 items to 6 goals with associated problems.

If a problem cannot be matched with any of the goals, consider discarding the problem if it is relatively unimportant, or create a new goal. A new goal would describe the desired outcome when the problem has been solved. For example, a problem may be the inability to meet delivery deadlines, or the fact that 75 percent of the organization's resources is spent on rework. Related goals may be meeting deadlines 100 percent of the time, or reducing rework to 25 percent. It is not necessary to have problems for each goal.

Table 1–1 Problems and Goals Grouped According to Which Problems Prevent Each Goal

Goal	Problem	Problem Description
1. Create predictable schedules.	Problem 7	Finding time to do critical activities (product development) is difficult. Time is spent on crisis activities.
	Problem 11	Revising the project plan is difficult. Items drop off, new things are added, plan is out of date.
	Problem 12	We don't understand our capacity and do not have one list of all the work we have to do.
	Problem 13	Schedule tracking and communication of changes to affected groups is poor.
	Problem 14	Testers do not have tools to manage their test activities.
2. Successfully deliver product X.	Problem 1	Need better requirements. Requirements tracking not in place. Changes to requirements are not tracked; code does not match specification at test time.
	Problem 2	Management direction unclear for product version 2.3. Goals change often.
3. Reduce rework.	Problem 3	Quality department does not have training in product and test skills.
	Problem 4	Unclear status of software changes.
	Problem 5	Lack of resources and skills allocated to software design.
	Problem 6	Changes to specifications and documentation are not communicated effectively to documentation and test groups.
	Problem 8	Test plan does not necessarily encompass things that matter to the customer.
	Problem 9	Defect repairs break essential product features.
	Problem 10	Wrong files (for example, dynamic link libraries) are put on CD. Unsure of the correct ones.

Goal	Problem	Problem Description
4. Improve the performance of our core software product.		
5. Keep customers happy.	Problem 15	Customers are unhappy. There are approximately 300 outstanding defects that have not been addressed.
6. Keep making a profit.		

Step 4: Ensure That the Goals and Problems Are Crystal Clear and Compelling

When you write your goals and problems, ensure that they are clear and concise. Some of the goals in Table 1–1 have been reworded for clarity in Table 1–2. The changes are shown using the strikeout feature of a word processor.

Table 1–2   Goals Reworded for Clarity

Goal	Problem	Problem Description
1. ~~Create predictable schedules.~~ Meet all our cost and schedule commitments.	Problem 7	Finding time to do critical activities (product development) is difficult. Time is spent on crisis activities.
	Problem 11	Revising the project plan is difficult. Items drop off, new things are added, plan is out of date.
	Problem 12	We don't understand our capacity and do not have one list of all the work we have to do.
	Problem 13	Schedule tracking and communication of changes to affected groups is poor.
	Problem 14	Testers do not have tools to manage their test activities. *continued*

Table 1–2   Goals Reworded for Clarity   *continued*

Goal	Problem	Problem Description
2. ~~Successfully deliver product X.~~ Deliver product X by mm/dd/yy.	Problem 1	Need better requirements. Requirements tracking not in place. Changes to requirements are not tracked; code does not match specification at test time.
	Problem 2	Management direction unclear for product version 2.3. Goals change often.
3. ~~Reduce rework.~~ Reduce rework to less than 20 percent of total project effort.	Problem 3	Quality department does not have training in product and test skills.
	Problem 4	Unclear status of software changes.
	Problem 5	Lack of resources and skills allocated to software design.
	Problem 6	Changes to specifications and documentation are not communicated effectively to documentation and test groups.
	Problem 8	Test plan does not necessarily encompass things that matter to the customer.
	Problem 9	Defect repairs break essential product features.
	Problem 10	Wrong files (for example, data link libraries) are put on CD. Unsure of the correct ones.
4. Improve the performance of our core software product. (Target to be defined.)		
5. ~~Keep customers happy.~~ Achieve customer rating of 9/10 on product evaluation form.	Problem 15	Customers are unhappy. There are approximately 300 outstanding defects that have not been addressed.

Goal	Problem	Problem Description
6. ~~Keep making a profit.~~ Keep profits at 15 percent (and costs at the same level as last year).		

The lack of a compelling purpose is a common reason for an organization to abandon its improvement program. Improving an organization and maintaining momentum requires an acute desire for each change. Such desire occurs when the change solves a high-priority problem or achieves a critical goal. Examples of compelling goals are the following:

- Increase product quality to a maximum of ten defects per release, gaining back customers X, Y, and Z, and increasing our market share by ten percent.
- Reduce rework to five percent of project effort. Use that time to create new product Y.
- Improve schedule prediction to ±five-day accuracy, eliminating forced cancellation of vacations.

Examples of goals that are *not* compelling are the following:

- Document all processes.
- Develop a detailed software life cycle.
- Establish a metrics program.

If your organization currently has process-related improvement goals that are not compelling, make them more so by asking, Why do I want to achieve this goal? This question elicits the benefits expected from achieving that goal. The most important benefit should become the new goal. You can either discard the original goal or make it an intermediate goal.

One of our clients set a goal to achieve CMM Level 3, but it was obvious that their lack of motivation was causing chronic procrastination. Their focus was made compelling by asking the question, Why do you want to achieve CMM Level 3? Their response was the following:

- Find defects early during the coding phase to reduce test costs.
- Reduce the $2 million currently spent on rework each year.
- Win more contracts by lowering rework costs.
- Improve schedule and cost predictability.
- Reduce schedule delays resulting from unmanaged risks in complex projects.
- Improve systems engineering and simplify product integration.

These benefits were far more important and compelling than the original goal. From this list, the group selected, *Reduce the $2 million currently spent on rework each year*, as its primary improvement goal. The other benefits, and the practices described by Level 3, became activities to support this goal.

When you seek goals that are compelling, expect your stakeholders to be motivated by different issues. Don't expect each stakeholder to have the same level of passion about each goal or problem in the plan. This is a very unlikely occurrence. Do, however, ensure that the plan encompasses each stakeholder's issues and be certain to follow through on each of them.

Step 5: Set Goal Priorities

Setting priorities and focusing on a few goals at a time is essential, especially if you have numerous goals and limited time for improvement. Establish the priority of each goal by considering its relative value and cost compared with other goals on the list. The following steps help establish priorities:

1. Using a 1-to-10-point scale, estimate the relative benefit of achieving the goal for the organization (1 = low, 10 = high).

   Consider the benefit of achieving each goal and rate each goal in order, relative to the other goals on the list. If you have benefit-specific data for each goal (for example, likely revenue, increased profit or reduced cost), use this information instead of the relative number.

2. Using a 1-to-10-point scale, estimate the relative cost of implementing the improvements related to this goal (1 = low, 10 = high).

   The relative cost can be based on a monetary or effort estimate required to accomplish the improvements for the goal. This number is an estimate of the relative cost compared with the other goals on the list. Revise the estimate as you refine the plan and add further detail.

3. Determine the priority of each goal (benefit divided by cost).

   Sorting the list using the priority calculation helps you determine your improvement focus. The accuracy of the priority number is not critical. Its purpose is to encourage you to think carefully about where your focus should be.

4. Look for goal interdependencies, logical ordering, and timing. Record this ordering by assigning a sequence number to each goal (for example, phase 1, phase 2, and phase 3).

This step makes the plan manageable by spreading the goals out over time. By assigning phases, you can incorporate dependencies between the goals, or the logical order of each goal, into the action plan. Phases could also indicate the required time frame when each goal needs to be achieved, such as the first or last quarter of the year.

Table 1–3 shows an example of a prioritization scheme. Goals have been sorted by the *Phase* column first and then by the *Priority* column. The improvement program would start with the highest priority items in phase 1.

Step 6: Derive Metrics for the Goals

Before you get too far into your improvement program, knowing how you are going to measure the program's effectiveness is key. Defining metrics for your goals helps you clarify objective criteria for goal completion. The discovery process of establishing metrics helps you understand your goals better and provides measurement actions to include in your final action plan. Expect to revisit these definitions several times as you progress through your improvement program. Defining an initial set of metrics is straightforward; defining a good set of metrics is not.

You can use the Goal-Question-Metric (GQM) approach from [Basili84] to derive metrics from goals. The GQM approach states that you

- Define the principal goals for your activity
- Construct a comprehensive set of questions that, when answered, helps assess where you are relative to each goal
- Define and gather the data required to answer these questions

Table 1–3   Setting Goal Priorities

Goal	Relative Benefit of Goal, 1–10 pts	Relative Cost of Goal, 1–10 pts	Priority (benefit/cost)	Phase
2. Deliver product X by mm/dd/yy.	10	4	2.5	1
Problem 1: Need better requirements. Requirements tracking not in place. Changes to requirements are not tracked; code does not match specification at test time.				
Problem 2: Management direction unclear for product version 2.3. Goals change often.				
1. Meet all our cost and schedule commitments.	9	5	1.8	1
Problem 7: Finding time to do critical activities (product development) is difficult. Time is spent on crisis activities.				
Problem 11: Revising the project plan is difficult. Items drop off, new things are added, plan is out of date.				
Problem 12: We don't understand our capacity and do not have one list of all the work we have to do.				
Problem 13: Schedule tracking and communication of changes to affected groups is poor.				
Problem 14: Testers do not have tools to manage their test activities.				
5. Achieve customer rating of 9/10 on product evaluation form.	6	6	1	1
Problem 15: Customers are unhappy. There are approximately 300 outstanding defects that have not been addressed.				

continued

Table 1–3 Setting Goal Priorities *continued*

Goal	Relative Benefit of Goal, 1–10 pts	Relative Cost of Goal, 1–10 pts	Priority (benefit/cost)	Phase
3. Reduce rework to less than 20 percent of total project effort.	7	5	1.4	2
Problem 3: Quality department does not have training in product and test skills.				
Problem 4: Unclear status of software changes.				
Problem 5: Lack of resources and skills allocated to software design.				
Problem 6: Changes to specifications and documentation are not communicated effectively to documentation and test groups.				
Problem 8: Test plan does not necessarily encompass things that matter to the customer.				
Problem 9: Defect repairs break essential product features.				
Problem 10: Wrong files (for example, dynamic link libraries) are put on CD. Unsure of the correct ones.				
6. Keep profits at 15 percent (and costs at the same level as last year).	9	5	1.8	3
4. Improve the performance of our core software product. (Target to be defined.)	5	7	0.7	3

The principal goals from which to derive metrics in this context are the business goals established earlier in this chapter. Constructing questions provides a stepping-stone to help you develop metrics. Table 1–4 uses this approach for some of the goals described in this book. In Chapter 3, we give examples of using these metrics to track improvement progress.

Using the Goal-Problem Approach for a Single Project
You can also use the goal-problem approach to scope an improvement program for an individual project. For example, one project leader had established the scope of her improvement program as "Achieve the characteristics of SEI CMM Level 3." By asking for a significant business goal, we helped her refocus the scope. By asking two additional questions related to this goal, we derived problem areas that needed improvement. This goal and the related problems formed the scope of the improvement program for this project (Figure 1–5).

What is your goal?
Reduce product development cycle to six to nine months for product X.

What is preventing you from achieving the goal (in other words, problems)?
1. Changing requirements
2. Loss of resources; difficult to replace people with specialized skills who leave the project
3. Too many features for the six- to nine-month development cycle
4. Poor quality of incoming code from other groups
5. Inadequate availability of test equipment

What other problems do you have related to this goal?
6. Lack of visibility within each life cycle phase. It is difficult to know whether we are ahead or behind schedule.
7. Don't always have the resources available to complete the planned work.
8. Difficult to find defects early.

Figure 1–5   Project-level improvement scope.

Table 1–4 The GQM Approach to Defining Metrics

Goal	Questions	Metrics
Meet all our cost and schedule commitments.	Are we spending the planned number of hours on the project to complete it? Are we hitting our milestones?	Planned versus actual effort for each project. The number of days each milestone is early or late.
Deliver product X by mm/dd/yy.	Are we spending the planned number of hours on the project to complete it? Are we hitting our milestones?	Planned vs. actual effort for each project milestone. The number of days each milestone is early or late
Reduce rework to less than 20 percent of total project effort.	How much time do we spend on rework now? How does this compare with our development time and are we improving?	Percentage of project time spent on rework
	How many defects do we have in the product during design and coding?	Defect density: number of defects found per unit size of work product (for example, number of pages of design, number of lines of code)
Improve the performance of our core software product. (Target to be defined.)	What is our current performance?	Average screen response time during peak system usage
Achieve customer rating of 9/10 on product evaluation form.	How satisfied are they now? Are we improving?	Annual customer satisfaction survey[2]
Keep profits at 15 percent (and costs at the same level as last year).	What is our profit? Is it getting better or worse?	Annual net profit

2. See [Cassell92, Westfall99] for further reading on measuring customer satisfaction.

This new scope was more compelling to her than "Achieve the characteristics of SEI CMM Level 3." The problems provided specific issues to address that had immediate benefit to her project and the organization. She used the practices in the CMM to solve these problems. Later in this chapter we show you how to integrate the CMM, or any other framework, with your improvement plan.

Using a Process Assessment to Obtain a Good Problem List

In the first scoping example (Figure 1–4), the list of goals and problems was obtained by having a group of developers and managers use a brainstorming technique. After the brainstorm, each element was discussed and reworded for clarity. In the second example (Figure 1–5), the problem list was derived from interviewing an individual project manager. These techniques were appropriate because only a handful of people were involved. Consensus could be easily reached. When the size of an organization is between 30 and 200 people, a process assessment is usually more effective at eliciting the key problems. Groups larger than 200 are best assessed in logical groups of 200 people or fewer.

A process assessment is a series of fact-finding interviews that identify the strengths and weaknesses related to how an organization develops and maintains software. The topic of assessments is covered well in the literature [Zahran98]. A typical process assessment

- Takes between one day and two weeks to complete, depending on the size of the organization, and whether an improvement framework is used

- Is conducted by a small assessment team consisting of developers and a trained assessment leader

- Results in a list of strengths and a focused list of critical problem areas challenging the organization

- Includes confidentiality rules, enabling the interviewees to be candid
- Contains reviews with the interviewees (developers and managers), ensuring agreement on the final findings

Grouping the problems (or areas for improvement) that prevent each business goal from being achieved maps the assessment findings to the business goals of the organization. In Figure 1–6, a sample set of problems from an assessment has been grouped under the three business goals of an organization.

You should now have a compelling set of goals and problems that define the scope of your improvement program. The plan has an owner and you have set priorities for the goals. The plan is still too high-level to execute, however, which leads us to the next step: *Develop an action plan.*

Business   Assessment
goal   finding

1. **Deliver on product development date estimates and costs.**
   Merged projects from outside the organization use different processes, making communication cumbersome (for example, software configuration management, estimation, schedules), leading to unplanned consumption of resources.

2. **Deliver on product development functionality.**
   Inadequate collaboration with the marketing department in developing business case and market analysis. Requests and product planning are short term and reactive.

3. **Maintain product quality.**
   Lack of focus on design/architecture issues

   - Necessary design practices have not been identified.
   - Inadequate time allocated for current design activities.
   - Coding starts before related design complete.

   Risk of losing control over software configuration management as organization grows, and as multiple products are built off the same platform.

Figure 1–6   Mapping assessment findings to business goals.

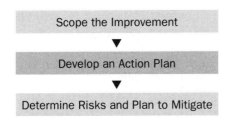

DEVELOP AN ACTION PLAN

Once you have determined goal priorities, your next step is to develop a detailed action plan. An action plan helps you

- Break each goal into smaller, manageable tasks
- Identify the most appropriate tasks and sequence that will achieve the desired goals
- Determine feedback points to monitor progress
- Think ahead, so the benefits and consequences of each action are considered before it is performed
- Communicate the actions and priorities to others who are affected

To develop an action plan, follow these steps:

1. Enumerate actions using brainstorming and a process framework.
2. Organize the action plan based on the goals and problems.
3. Add placeholders for checking progress and taking corrective action.

Step 1: Enumerate Actions Using Brainstorming and a Process Framework

Developing an action plan can be challenging. In the previous steps you identified specific problems that prevented the achievement of each goal. Use the following questions to develop actions for your plan.

- What actions are needed to address the problems and achieve the goals?

- If a process improvement framework is being used, which elements will help the problems and goals listed?

What Actions Are Needed to Address the Problems and Achieve the Goals?

Earlier in this chapter (in Figure 1–5), we gave an example of a product cycle-time goal. Table 1–5 shows actions for two of the related problems. You can develop such actions by brainstorming with a group of colleagues or project team members.

If a Process Improvement Framework Is Being Used, Which Elements Will Help the Problems and Goals Listed?

If you are using an improvement framework, choose individual elements from the reference material that address the problems and goals. With ISO9001, look for small pieces that specifically address your problems; don't select one whole section of the standard. Similarly with the CMM, select individual activities

Table 1–5   Actions for Two of the Project's Problems

Problem	What Actions Are Needed to Address the Problems and Achieve the Goals?
1. Changing requirements	• Baseline the requirements before design commences. • Only allow changes to the application interface, not to the kernel routines. • Improve the library control system to minimize version control errors. • Investigate requirements management tools.
3. Too many features for the six- to nine-month development cycle	• Establish a review process with clients to negotiate features for a six- to nine-month development cycle. • Rate each feature based on value to the customer (1–10 points) and cost to develop (1–10 points). • Establish an incremental delivery plan to phase in lower priority features.

that are appropriate; don't select a whole section of practices at one time.

For example, when solving the first problem in Table 1–5, the majority of the requirements management section of the CMM (12 individual items) could be used. Adopting all 12 at once would be overwhelming. Instead, select two or three practices with which to start. In Table 1–6, we show examples of activities from the CMM (reworded for clarity) for problems 1 and 3. If you are using another improvement framework, select appropriate elements that help you solve the problems on which you

Table 1–6 Examples of Using Elements from CMM 1.1 for Two of the Project Problems

Problem	If a Process Improvement Framework Is Being Used, Which Elements Will Help the Problems Listed? (examples from CMM 1.1)
1. Changing requirements	◆ Review the initial requirements and changes before they are incorporated into the project plan (based on CMM Requirements Management activity 1). ◆ Establish a group with the authority for managing the project's software baselines (based on CMM Software Configuration Management ability 1). ◆ Record and track change requests and problem reports for all configuration items (based on CMM Software Configuration Management activity 5).
3. Too many features for the six- to nine-month development cycle	◆ Review project commitments with senior managers, software engineers, and the customer to obtain agreement (based on CMM Software Project Planning activity 4). ◆ Perform risk management related to the schedule, resource, and technical aspects of the project (based on CMM Software Project Planning activity 13).

are focusing. Appendices A and B contain additional mapping examples.

Applying elements from the framework to each problem provides a real-life context for using these elements. The framework is not implemented by writing procedures and then determining how to use them (process-centric approach). It is implemented piece by piece to solve the real problems of the organization.

Observe the Alignment Between Your Planned Actions and Chosen Improvement Framework

Some people worry that, with the goal-problem approach, an organization will not achieve its initial goal (such as CMM Level 3 or ISO9001) because its attention will be diverted to the business goals and problems lists. To avoid this outcome, after addressing the first set of problems and goals, repeat the planning cycle to determine the next set of problems and goals. This new set can then be compared with the remaining elements in the framework. In this way, over time, each section of the framework can be matched with a problem or goal.

In the example in Figure 1–4, 20 of the 21 items map to CMM Level 2 practices (see mapping in Appendix A). Addressing all these problems and goals results in 43 percent[3] of the Level 2 practices being adopted. After 11 months, the organization that is cited in this example conducted an informal process assessment to monitor its progress. The assessment showed that, in fact, 50 percent of CMM Level 2 practices had been adopted.

At the end of the assessment, the group revised its problem list for its next improvement phase. The problems were the following:

◆ Files on CDs delivered to the customer are not verified.

---

3. Calculation is based on a count of 99 distinct practices in SEI CMM Level 2 (v1.1), excluding Software Subcontract Management.

- Actual data is not recorded from the initial project plan to determine how well we did.

- We don't know the status of our testing activities and when we are ready to ship.

- We don't know the specific differences between one software release and the previous release.

- We don't verify that the processes we have put in place are used correctly.

Each one of these items maps specifically to further practices in the SEI CMM.

In some situations, certain framework elements are not used when solving a problem or achieving a goal. Adoption of such elements should be delayed until the end of the improvement cycle. At that time, these outstanding elements are either put to good use or considered "not applicable."

Elements are put to good use by asking the question: What problem could this element help solve? For example, baseline audits are included in some frameworks under the topic of Software Configuration Management (SCM). A baseline audit verifies that the files in a software product release are indeed the correct ones. The audit can be accomplished by verifying file version numbers, file sizes, and filenames, or by comparing checksum counts with the original file set. This element in the framework is often ignored because it is not obvious why it is needed. Asking "What problem could this element help solve?" may elicit project team experiences when the wrong files were sent to the testing group or released to the customer. Baseline audits help solve these problems. Asking this question not only elicits a good reason to perform this new practice, but also enables you to implement the practice in a way that is customized to the organization's needs.

The goal-problem approach also helps an organization avoid prematurely using practices from an improvement framework. Process auditing is one example of a practice that is sometimes adopted prematurely. Process audits verify that the correct process steps have been carried out when performing activities such as schedule estimation, testing, peer reviews, and SCM. Process audits identify and eliminate engineering and management mistakes before they cause large, unnecessary downstream costs. In the beginning of an improvement program, there is usually little benefit in performing process audits because engineering and management activities have not yet been defined. However, the need for auditing a process becomes apparent once a process has been defined and used.

One company realized the need for auditing while using its software release management process. Before release management had been improved, performing an audit on related SCM activities would have been futile. After release management practices were put in place, an employee bypassed the process and incorrectly released a software patch by e-mail to a customer, who became furious when the software did not work. At that point, the need for SCM auditing became apparent. After the audits were performed, developers and managers realized that they now had a mechanism to verify execution of the defined release management activities.

Step 2: Organize the Action Plan Based on the Goals and Problems

The format in Figure 1–7 is one suggested way of organizing the action plan.[4] The figure displays the information visually so that it is clear which actions support each goal.

---

4. The action plan format is based on Anthony Robbins *The Time of Your Life* audio program [Robbins98].

Action Plan Owner: _____

Primary Goal and Intermediate Goals (The result you want)	Purpose of Goal (Why do you want to achieve this goal?)	Actions	Priority (*essential)	Time Estimate	Who
PRIMARY GOAL 1	**PURPOSE OF PRIMARY GOAL 1**				
Small intermediate goal (based on problem statement)	Purpose of small intermediate goal	Action	1*		
		Action	2*		
		Action	3		
		Action	4		
Next intermediate goal	Purpose of next intermediate goal	Action	1*		

Figure 1–7 Action plan format.

The columns are defined as follows:

Primary Goal and Intermediate Goals: This column states the primary and intermediate goals of the improvement project. Each intermediate goal in the action plan is based on one problem statement. For example, the problem statement *Changing requirements* can be rewritten as an intermediate goal *Manage changing requirements.* The intermediate goal is a statement of the desired outcome when the problem has been solved. A complete list of the problems and derived intermediate goals is shown in Table 1–7.

Purpose of Goal: This column reminds you of your motive for this goal. The motive is determined by asking, Why do I want to achieve this goal? What benefit does it provide? Always complete this column. It will keep you focused and pull you through times when you are ready to give up.

Actions: This column lists all the actions that contribute to achieving the intermediate goal. Some of these are small; some of them are more involved and will need breaking up into further detail. If your improvement plan is for a group of projects or one large department, make each action specific to a project where it will be applied next. For example, the action *Interview customers to elicit requirements* can be restated as *Interview customers to elicit requirements for product J.* Being specific makes the plan meaningful and directly focused on someone's need. If there are other known recipients for this action, they can be added as separate actions. If other recipients have not been identified yet, you can identify them later as you deploy your improvements using the guidelines in Chapter 2.

Table 1–7 Problems Rewritten as Intermediate Goals

Original Problem	Problem Rewritten as an Intermediate Goal
1. Changing requirements	Manage changing requirements
2. Loss of resources; difficult to replace people with specialized skills who leave the project	Replace people with specialized skills who leave the project
3. Too many features for the six- to nine-month development cycle	Set feature priorities for a six- to nine-month development cycle
4. Poor quality of incoming code from other groups	Improve quality of incoming code from other groups
5. Inadequate availability of test equipment	Ensure adequate availability of test equipment
6. Lack of visibility within each life cycle phase. It is difficult to know whether we are ahead or behind schedule	Improve visibility within all life cycle phases
7. Don't always have the resources available to complete the planned work	Ensure resources are available to complete the planned work
8. Difficult to find defects early	Find defects earlier

Priority: This column records the priority of your actions. For each intermediate goal, mark approximately 20 percent of the actions with an asterisk. If there are only five or six actions in the list, mark two or three. Focus on the ones that you believe will help you make the greatest progress toward the intermediate goal. Your focus should be on achieving the intermediate goal you stated, not necessarily on doing all of the actions.

Time Estimate: This column is for an estimate of the time required for completing the action. The column can be totaled to determine how much time is required for each intermediate goal.

Who: This column is for the name of the person responsible for completing the action.

Step 3: Add Placeholders for Checking Progress and Taking Corrective Action

When executing your action plan, periodic checks assess whether your primary and intermediate goals are being addressed. Add a placeholder for this activity in your action plan at the end of the actions marked with an asterisk (Figure 1–8). After these essential actions are complete, determine whether the intermediate goal has been adequately addressed. If not, execute the next one or two actions in the plan and check again. Your focus should be on achieving the intermediate goal you stated, not necessarily on completing all of the actions.

In Chapter 3 we discuss other methods of checking progress, using the metrics you constructed at the end of the planning phase. These will help you better evaluate the progress you have made.

Action Plan Example

Here is an example of an action plan using this format (Figure 1–8[5]). The main goal is *Reduce product development cycle to six to nine months for product X.* The intermediate goals have been derived from problems previously identified. Further detail for this action plan is described in Appendix C.

---

5. A template of this plan is available at www.processgroup.com/bookinfo.htm.

Action Plan Owner: Jane

Primary Goal and Intermediate Goals (The results you want)	Purpose of Goal (Why do you want to achieve the goal?)	Actions	Priority (*essential)	Time Estimate	Who
Reduce product development cycle to six to nine months for product X.	Deliver earlier than competition.				
Manage changing requirements (based on problem 1).	Prevent schedule slips resulting from expensive scope changes.	Only allow changes to the application interface, not to the kernel routines.	1*	4 hrs	Jane
		Establish a group with the authority for managing the project's software baselines.	2*	4 hrs	Pradeep
		Check progress and take corrective action.[6]	—	2 hrs	Jane
		Improve the library control system to minimize version control errors. Investigate requirements management tools.	3	80 hrs	Fred

continued

6. This is a placeholder for the activities described in Chapter 3.

Figure 1–8 Action plan example.

Primary Goal and Intermediate Goals (The results you want)	Purpose of Goal (Why do you want to achieve the goal?)	Actions	Priority (*essential)	Time Estimate	Who
		Record and track change requests and problem reports for all configuration items.	4	2 hrs/week	Jane
		Review the initial requirements and changes before they are incorporated into the project plan.	5	2 hrs/week	Mike
		Baseline the requirements before design commences.	6	20 hrs	Jane
Set feature priorities for a six- to nine-month development cycle (based on problem 3).	Ensure commitments are achievable.	Establish a review process with clients to negotiate features for a 6- to 9-month development cycle.	1*	16 hrs	Jane
		Rate each feature based on value to the customer (1–10 points) and cost to develop (1–10 points).	2*	4 hrs	Jim
		Check progress and take corrective action.[7]	—	2 hrs	Jim

7. This is a placeholder for the activities described in Chapter 3.

Primary Goal and Intermediate Goals (The results you want)	Purpose of Goal (Why do you want to achieve the goal?)	Actions	Priority (*essential)	Time Estimate	Who
		Review project commitments with senior managers, engineers, and the customer to obtain agreement.	3	2 hrs	Kim
		Perform risk management related to the schedule, resource, and technical aspects of the project.	4	2 hrs	B.J.
		Establish an incremental delivery plan to phase in lower priority features.	5	3 hrs	Jim

Figure 1–8   Action plan example *(continued)*.

Choose Actions That Are Appropriate for the Problem

Occasionally, engineers and managers select unnecessarily complex or inappropriate solutions, and then waste time and money trying to get them to work. Examples are shown in Table 1–8. The solutions, by themselves, are good solutions; however, each is a poor match for the problems listed.

In the first example, quality function deployment (QFD) is a technique for relating product features and attributes to customer value [Wiegers99]. QFD is more rigorous than needed for this problem. In the second example, adopting a detailed design process does not change the fact that inadequate time is allocated for design. Adopting a design technique would amplify the problem. Similarly, building a database to store estimation data on four platforms serves little purpose when current estimates are inaccurate. In this particular company, there was no estimation technique defined and no historical data to store. (Building a database was fun though!) In the last example, the quality problem was the result of numerous coding mistakes and inadequate testing. Defining a complete life cycle is a good

Table 1–8 Inappropriate and Unnecessarily Complex Solutions

Problem	Inappropriate and Overly Complex Solution
Unable to get requirements from customers	Adopt quality function deployment— a highly systematic technique for relating product features and attributes to customer value.
No time allocated for design	Adopt a detailed object-oriented design process.
Inaccurate estimates	Create a new historical database, built from scratch, and available on four platforms.
Poor-quality software products	Define a detailed software life cycle, containing numerous software engineering methods.

long-term strategy, but it is not appropriate for the current problem. Simpler solutions, and ones focused on the problems, are shown in Table 1–9.

When you create your action plan in collaboration with others, keep a keen eye on the complexity of the proposed actions and their appropriateness to the problems being solved. Heavy-

Table 1–9 Simpler Solutions Focused on the Problems

Problem	Simpler Solution
Unable to get requirements from customers	◆ Establish a primary customer liaison. ◆ Interview the customers. ◆ Develop a prototype of the product showing customers what features are possible.
No time allocated for design	◆ Clarify what "design" means in our environment. ◆ Estimate the time needed for the design phase. ◆ Learn negotiation techniques for obtaining time in the schedule for design. ◆ Allocate time for designing the highest risk product components.
Inaccurate estimates	◆ Learn an estimation process that addresses some of the root causes of the inaccurate estimates (for example, the Wideband Delphi method). ◆ Start collecting actual data for current projects so that they can compare their estimates with actual effort expended.
Poor-quality software products	◆ Inspect (peer review) all critical documents and code. ◆ Improve estimation of test time needed. ◆ Train test engineers in test skills. ◆ Send test engineers to a customer site to understand how the customer uses the product. Factor this knowledge into the test strategy.

weight, all-encompassing, and new-technology solutions are not necessarily what you need. Be wary of grand schemes, such as building a robot to collect data from the estimation team and put it into a relational database, when a laptop set up in the conference room would work just fine!

You should now have a compelling and comprehensive action plan for your improvement program. If you are using an improvement framework, you have used elements from this to populate your action plan. The plan, however, does contain risks and surprises that need addressing. These concealed potholes are addressed by the next step: *Determine risks and plan to mitigate.*

DETERMINE RISKS AND PLAN TO MITIGATE

Risk management is similar to preventive health care and insurance for your improvement project. It involves identifying risks (making potential problems visible), analyzing those risks, managing them, and reviewing them. When risk management techniques are used, you can prevent problems and anticipate others, making your improvement project run smoothly [Boehm89, Potter01, Van Scoy92].

The risk process described here is simple, effective and typically takes 90 to 120 minutes for improvement projects with 12 to 24 person-months of effort. Projects smaller than 12 person-months can take less time. You can control the length of the session by controlling the scope you pick. Most sessions take less than two hours.

There are six steps in our risk management process. A description of the process follows.

Step 1: Determine the Scope of the Risk Session

The scope of the risk session can be the complete list of goals and problems in your action plan, or just the few on which you plan to work in the near term. The goals and problems you plan to address in the next six months would be a reasonable scope.

Step 2: Select the Team and Moderator

Invite individuals who can suggest risks that may prevent the successful completion of the improvement project. Invite the improvement team, your stakeholders (for example, software developers, software quality analysts, and managers), people who have been on similar improvement projects, and experts in the subject area. Limit the group size to nine people to keep the discussion focused.

Assign a moderator to keep the session on track. The moderator explains the risk process to new team members unfamiliar with the scope of the risk session or the risk management process.

Step 3: Identify Risks

Risks are *potential* problems, ones that are not guaranteed to occur. A brainstorming session is an effective way of identifying risks. The session typically takes 15 to 30 minutes. During the session, people call out potential problems that they think could cause the project to fail.

When performing risk identification, team members often start by listing known problems. Known problems are not risks. If this occurs, just move them to a problem list and concentrate on future *potential* problems (ones not currently occurring or not guaranteed to occur). During the brainstorm, consider the following items:

- ♦ Weak areas such as unknown technology; for example, tools, vendors, and methods that are new to the team

◆ Aspects that are critical to the improvement project, such as the timely delivery of a vendor's training program, continued buy-in from management, and the creation of training materials

◆ Problems that have plagued past projects, such as loss of essential staff, resistance to change, and changing priorities

Examples of risks include: "We may not have captured the most important business goals," "The new method is untested," "Key people might leave," and "People might resist the change." Any potential problem is a good candidate for the risk list. Once you have created a list, work with the group to remove duplicate items.

Step 4: Analyze Risks

The first task in analyzing risks is removing ambiguities and ensuring that each team member understands each risk item. Risks such as "Lack of management buy-in" and "People might leave" are ambiguous. In these cases, the group may decide to split the risk into smaller specific risks such as "Manager Jane could decide that the new method is not beneficial," "Test expert might leave," and "Web master might get pulled off the project."

The second task in analyzing risks is enumerating the primary consequence if the risk occurred. This discussion allows the team members to understand each other's perspectives of the risk and to be better prepared to assign an impact number during the next task. The primary consequence of each risk is captured in the *Consequence* column (see Table 1–10).

The last task sets priorities and helps you determine where to focus your risk mitigation efforts. Some of the identified risks are unlikely to occur and others may not be serious enough to worry about. For example, if there is a risk of a key person leaving, you may decide that it would have a large impact on the project, but that it is not very likely.

Set priorities by agreeing as a team how likely each risk item is to occur, using a scale from 1 to 10 (where 1 is very unlikely and 10 is very likely). Then rate how serious the impact would be if the risk did occur, using a scale from 1 to 10 (where 1 is a small impact and 10 is a very large impact). To use this numbering scheme, first select the items that rate 1, then select the items that rate 10, and then rate the remaining items relative to these boundaries.

The priority of each risk item is the product of the two values: likelihood multiplied by impact. This priority scheme helps push the big risks to the top of the list and the small risks to the bottom. Table 1–10 gives an example.

An alternative rating process is to use absolute numbers that reflect impact and likelihood. For example, using a time or cost impact assessment of each risk item would lead you to a more precise rating, assuming you have accurate data. Similarly, using historical probability data (instead of a likelihood number) would also increase your precision. If you don't have any historical data (and most people don't), use the rating system provided. The intent of the rating system is to focus you on a few critical risk areas. For that, a precise rating system is not required.

Now that the group has assigned a priority to each risk, select a few items to manage. Some project teams pursue a few of the risk actions, whereas others choose to work on all of them. Start by selecting the top three risks, or the top 20 percent, based on the priority calculation.

Step 5: Plan to Mitigate

The first way to manage risk is by reducing the likelihood of the risk occurring. For example, some improvement teams set their deadlines earlier to minimize the likelihood of team members

Table 1-10 Example of Risks for an Improvement Project

Risk Items (Potential future problems derived from the brainstorming session)	Consequence if Risk Item Does Occur	Likelihood of Risk Item Occurring	Impact to Project if Risk Item Does Occur	Priority (Likelihood × Impact)
Management buy-in for improvement diminishes.	Improvement program fails.	9	10	90
Management changes priorities before we complete any milestone.	Improvement program loses credibility.	9	9	81
New requirements management tool has long learning curve.	Developers give up in frustration.	9	8	72
Library control person might leave.	Wasted time training a new person.	7	8	56
New group to manage baseline changes is not accepted by project managers.	Duplication of effort, or baseline changes are not managed.	6	9	54
Creation of specialized training materials for new staff takes too long.	Improvement implementation delayed.	5	7	35
Requirements management tool is delivered to us late.	Pass up the opportunity to try the tool.	4	3	12

being pulled off the project as a result of changing organizational priorities. They increase the number of dedicated hours on the project during this shorter time period to complete the project. Another example would be for an improvement project to obtain a demonstration copy of a vendor tool early, so that the learning curve can be started earlier.

For some risks, consider eliminating the likelihood altogether by changing the decision that caused the risk. For example, the risk *Creation of specialized training materials for new staff takes too long* only exists because of the decision to create specialized training materials. Changing this decision will change its likelihood to zero and effectively eliminate it. An alternate option that may have less inherent risk is to contract the work out or license existing materials from an external group.

The second way to manage risk is by taking action to reduce the impact if the risk does occur. This involves starting the contingency in preparation for the risk. For example, to prepare for the potential loss of a key person, ensure that other team members become familiar with that person's work, or identify backup resources that can take over should the risk occur. Similarly, if a vendor's requirements tool is late, establish a manual process to manage requirements changes until the tool arrives.

Further examples are shown in the risk management plan for the top three risks (Table 1–11[8]). The right side of the table includes additional columns for assigning and tracking the action items.

Once you have developed risk management actions, decide which of them you are going to pursue. We suggest that you start by implementing a few actions for each selected risk. Focus on actions that reduce the likelihood of the risk, but also

---

8. A template of this plan is available at www.processgroup.com/bookinfo.htm.

Table 1–11 Risk Management Plan to Mitigate the Top Three Risks

Risk Items (Potential future problems derived from the brainstorming session)	Consequence if Risk Item Does Occur	Likelihood of Risk Item Occurring	Impact to Project if Risk Item Does Occur	Priority (Likelihood × Impact)	Actions to Reduce Likelihood of Risk Occurring	Actions to Reduce Impact if Risk Does Occur	Who is Responsible for These Actions?	When Actions Should be Complete	Status of Action
Management buy-in for improvement diminishes.	Improvement program fails.	9	10	90	1. Ensure that the improvement program addresses the management team's problems and goals. 2. Establish a steering committee to oversee the improvement effort. Meet bimonthly.	4. Determine improvements that can be made at a project level without major funding. 5. Explain the problems and goals that will not be addressed because of reduced funding.	Action 1: Joe Action 2: Jill	3/3/YY 4/3/YY	Complete Complete

Management changes priorities before we complete any milestone.	Improvement program loses credibility.	9	9	81	1. Present the action plan to management and obtain agreement that priorities remain unchanged between major improvement milestones. 2. Explain the problems and goals that will not be addressed if changes in priority occur.	3. Determine improvements that can be made regardless of which project is active.	3. Provide four funding options for the improvement program: full-time, part-time, short bursts, and investment spread over two years.	6. Determine a time when the improvement program can be revisited.	Action 1: Cathy	5/6/YY	In progress

continued

45

Table 1–11 Risk Management Plan to Mitigate the Top Three Risks *continued*

Risk Items (Potential future problems derived from the brainstorming session)	Consequence if Risk Item Does Occur	Likelihood of Risk Item Occurring	Impact to Project if Risk Item Does Occur	Priority (Likelihood × Impact)	Actions to Reduce Likelihood of Risk Occurring	Actions to Reduce Impact if Risk Does Occur	Who is Responsible for These Actions?	When Actions Should be Complete	Status of Action
New requirements management tool has long learning curve.	Developers give up in frustration.	9	8	72	1. Start a pilot project to test the tool. 2. Select a subset of the tool's features to use. 3. Have vendor come on-site to help transition to the tool.	4. Establish a cutoff date when we will give up on the tool and use manual methods instead. The tool can be used on the next release.	Action 1: Lois	4/6/YY	In progress

consider actions that provide the project with a contingency plan in case you are unable to prevent the risk. You may decide not to implement some actions because they are too costly. If the likelihood of the risk has not been reduced by the first action from the column labeled *Actions to Reduce Likelihood of Risk Occurring,* implement the next action from the column.

Using the Risk Information

The risk information in Table 1–11 is only useful if acted upon. There are four primary ways to integrate the risk information into your improvement action plan:

1. **Move high-risk actions earlier or later in the action plan.**
   Based on the risk information you have enumerated, change the sequence of the actions in the improvement plan by moving high-risk actions earlier or later. In Table 1-11, one of the identified risks was the learning curve of the new requirements management tool. The team can address this risk by ensuring that the tool is purchased and made operational earlier than originally stated. Alternatively, the team could delay purchase of the tool until adequate training is available.

2. **Add more detail to the areas of the action plan that have the highest risk.**
   High-risk areas can also be addressed by adding more detail to the related part of the improvement action plan. For example, selecting and buying a new requirements management tool has less risk if it is broken up into more detail. The following subtasks help reduce risk:
   - Obtain several references from existing tool users.
   - Select the most needed subset of the tool's features.
   - Invite vendors for tool demonstrations.
   - Establish a budget and purchase order.

  - ◆ Select one tool for evaluation using a pilot project.
  - ◆ Have a vendor come on-site to help transition to the tool.

3. **Add more time to the areas of the action plan that have the highest risk.**
The highest risk areas of any project will most likely take longer than planned. These delays can have a ripple effect on the remaining project milestones. Adding more time to the highest risk areas is one way to counter this effect. The final project deadline would only be impacted if these high-risk improvement actions were on the critical path (the longest path through the schedule).

4. **Add risk mitigation actions to the improvement action plan.**
During the risk session, team members propose mitigation actions for reducing risk likelihood and impact. Add the ones selected for implementation to the overall improvement action plan.

Step 6: Plan for Periodic Risk Review

Reviewing your risks periodically will provide visibility on how well mitigation is progressing. During these reviews, determine whether any risk likelihood or impact numbers need revising, if new risks have been discovered, or if any risk is no longer an issue. Many people incorporate risk review into other regularly scheduled project reviews. You may decide to repeat the complete risk process if significant changes have occurred on the project. Significant changes include adding new scope, changing the target platform of a tool, or changing project team members.

SUMMARY

Scoping and planning an improvement program can be difficult and frustrating. The task becomes daunting when a process framework is adopted wholesale; however, a simple solution exists. Using goals and problems provides a timeless and effective approach for scoping an improvement program. You can then use a framework as a source of ideas, solutions, and actions to achieve this scope. The resulting goal-problem improvement program is both compelling and practical.

The goal-problem approach has four significant benefits:

1. All improvements are tied to specific needs of the organization.

2. Goals and problems help the organization identify which pieces of an improvement framework to implement next. The goal-problem approach treats the framework as a large suite of little actions, ideas, and solutions, each of which is useful at different times.

3. Goals and problems establish the scope and context for each improvement. When a problem has been solved or a goal addressed, a team can stop defining the process or standard and focus on the next issue.

4. Developers and managers are motivated to work on improvement because the effort is directed toward the group's software development needs.

Quick Start

- Determine the primary business goals and problems of your group.

- Simplify the list of goals and problems by grouping the related problems under each goal.

- Verify that the scope of your improvement program is compelling. If not, ask: Why do I want to achieve these goals?

- Look at the goals and problems on which your improvement plan will be based. Pick one goal and use the GQM approach to determine the metrics you need to track progress toward this goal.

- Develop an action plan for the goal that you have selected.

- If you are using an improvement framework, use the goal and related problems to select the framework pieces that help you the most.

- Identify potential future problems (risks) with the action plan. Plan to mitigate the highest priority risks.

2

Implementing the Plan

"Proving that the true skeptics are indeed truly
skeptical achieves nothing, except that you've dented
your pick and probably permanently diminished your
credibility (and failed to appreciate the vital
importance of building a fragile momentum)."
—Tom Peters, *A Passion for Excellence*
[Peters85]

Now that you have spent some time planning your improvement effort, it is time to make those plans a reality. Implementing your plan may feel overwhelming. It includes building and deploying solutions, selling ideas, and overcoming resistance. In this chapter we provide guidance on how to proceed.

The four necessary guiding principles for action plan implementation are the following:

1. Sell solutions based on needs.

2. Work with the willing and needy first.

3. Keep focused on the goals and problems.

4. Align the behaviors of managers and practitioners.

SELL SOLUTIONS BASED ON NEEDS

Selling is required for all improvement progress. During the course of implementing your plan, you will need to sell ideas to many different people. This may include software developers, hardware developers, systems engineers, marketing people, and managers. You will need to convince them to try new practices, donate time, or contribute funding.

Many of us cringe at the thought of having to sell, but actually we sell our ideas all the time. Here is an exercise to demonstrate that you already know about selling. Recall a shopping trip when you had an exceptional experience with a salesperson, when you received perhaps the best treatment ever. Now write down some of the traits of the salesperson who made the experience so effective. Compare your list with the following items:

- Was helpful.
- Understood my needs and priorities.
- Didn't pressure me.
- Listened to my questions and gave me direct answers.
- Was knowledgeable about the product.
- Didn't sell me a more expensive item than I needed—allowed the product to sell itself.
- Offered a trial to evaluate the product.
- Gave me a fair price and a good return policy.
- Provided excellent postsale support.

Managers and developers all over the world provide us exactly the same answers when they describe the traits of an exceptional salesperson. These selling characteristics work because they focus on the customer's agenda rather than the salesperson's. At its core, the list focuses on the needs of the customer and comprehends the Golden Rule—paraphrased here as "Treat others as you would like to be treated." The rule applies whether you are selling to practitioners, managers, marketing people, or end users.

The easiest and most effective selling strategy is to solve one of your customer's problems. The list of good selling traits describes the style you should adopt during the sales process.

An Example of Selling

For this example let's assume that the manager with whom you are working was not involved in the initial improvement-planning phase and, therefore, some selling is needed. The following steps illustrate how to use the sales principles to gain a manager's support for improvement.

Step 1: Determine the manager's needs.

Step 2: Show how the improvement meets the manager's needs.

Step 3: Determine and address the manager's concerns and fears about improvement.

Step 4: Verify that improvement is meeting the manager's needs.

Step 1: Determine the Manager's Needs

Schedule a meeting with the manager to understand her problems and goals. This session will help you determine whether there is common ground for proceeding. For example, you could start by saying, "I have been helping other projects with risk management, schedule estimation, and product testing. I would like to see if I could help your group too. Would you tell me about your group, its goals, and any specific problems that you have?"

Some people have interviewed their manager with disappointing results. In hindsight, some of them skip the crucial step of listening to the needs of the manager. Instead, they immediately suggest an improvement program or solution. Determine the manager's needs and then offer a possible solution.

If there are no unmet needs, goals, or problems to solve, then mutually agree that nothing will be done. Forcing the issue would create a win-lose situation that would eventually become lose-lose. The good news is that most managers have numerous problems to solve, but you have to listen to discover what they are.

When managers reply to your question, they will describe symptoms that frustrate them. These symptoms usually involve project schedule, quality, and cost problems. Your next step is to help them determine some of the causes of those symptoms. For example, if they chronically overshoot schedules, ask them where things break down, resulting in this primary frustration. You may discover that the group has requirements management under control but lacks requirements clarity and is, therefore, unable to estimate well. Or the group may lack risk management and may suffer from numerous technical surprises on the project. Narrow down some likely causes. If the manager does not know why the symptom persists, ask if there is someone who can provide more detail on the day-to-day problems.

Step 2: Show How the Improvement Meets the Manager's Needs

Once the needs are well understood, it is time to suggest your improvement ideas and ask for comments. Focus on the aspects that will help the manager and the organization. Know your solutions thoroughly so that you can adapt them correctly to the needs that you have identified.

Be open about weak areas in your proposal. Most people will help you improve weaknesses when you have demonstrated an understanding of the problem. For example, if you know that your requirements elicitation solution has not been tested on groups with a geographically diverse customer base in different time zones, state that up front. Honesty about your solution will improve your credibility. Don't oversell your solution either. Remain conservative about its benefits. An overoptimistic salesperson loses credibility quickly, because no one believes all the claims made. A statement such as, "Your life will be changed forever with this new process" would be a turnoff!

Step 3: Determine and Address the Manager's Concerns and Fears About Improvement

The manager may be concerned that adopting your idea will result in pain or loss. You must understand and address these potential barriers. Because the improvement idea may be conceptually sound, but perceived as painful, you must show how to reduce the risk of pain. Options include further education, the addition of go/no-go decision points, and experimental improvements such as piloting the improvement with a willing and enthusiastic team. If the manager feels that she can maintain sufficient influence and significantly reduce the risk of pain, the idea will be more appealing.

For example, people sometimes associate improvement with teams of engineers who write time-wasting processes that inhibit creativity. If this is the belief, you will need to communicate otherwise. Emphasize that improvement should consist of identifying and solving the most important problems of the organization. Let the manager know that process documentation is not necessarily the result. You should always address current perceptions and fears about any proposed change.

Your job is to ensure that all improvements are concise and directly helpful to the manager and the organization. If the improvement is seen as academic, cumbersome, or documentation-centric, a manager will not support it for very long. If you understand her problems, you will be able to focus the improvement on a direct need. For example, one client asked us to help a development team in crisis. The team was tasked with configuring and deploying an e-mail/Web browser system for 2,000 users within a two-month schedule. The team currently had no plan for completing the goal. We took our standard project-planning workshop and stripped out most of the lecture material, leaving only the exercises. Over a two-day period, we coached the team on how to create a project plan, which they used to deliver the product on time. Listening carefully to the manager's needs allowed us to construct a lightweight solution that could be immediately applied.

Step 4: Verify That Improvement Is Meeting the Manager's Needs

While implementing improvements, ensure that they are meeting the manager's needs. If you make incremental changes and test them out, you can refine the new practices based on the results. For example, if you work on requirements management, pilot the idea on one small project that involves marketing and development. Report lessons learned and decide if progress is being made. You can then refine the solution before deploying it to other projects.

Selling the Same Thing More Than One Way

If you are using these selling techniques, you will find that often you will sell the same idea in multiple ways, depending on the needs of your customer. For example, if you wanted to introduce peer reviews [Gilb93] into your organization, first take some time to understand the current problems people are having. Let's say you find someone with support problems whose team is constantly drained by fixing existing software instead of working on new products. If you show them how they can significantly reduce this drain by using peer reviews on their current work, then they will be more interested in your peer review solution. If, on the other hand, you find someone who is primarily interested in mitigating current schedule pressures, your sales approach would be different. You might sell peer reviews by showing how products can ship sooner by quickly finding the majority of the defects before testing, allowing the test phase to proceed smoothly.

Selling is an important part of improvement. Little progress can be made without it. Listen to your customers' problems and provide tailored solutions using your expertise.

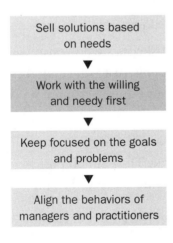

WORK WITH THE WILLING AND NEEDY FIRST

As you execute your action plan, you will discover that some people are not ready for change, whereas others cannot wait to get started. As much as you try to execute your plan in the intended sequence, you will probably complete little pieces of it in a different order, based on the needs of your audience. Well-executed improvement requires good timing and necessitates matching your solutions with the current needs of your customers.

When a new practice is deployed, you may see five groups during the adoption, as shown in Figure 2–1, adapted from *Diffusion of Innovations* [Rogers62].[1] The adoption curve described here and in Figure 2–1 is a tool for timing your execution to meet your organization's needs in the most pain-free manner.

Innovators: At the leading edge, you have a few individuals who may be perceived as early champions or fanatics. These are people who will try anything new or who have a desperate need for your solution.

Early Adopters: Early adopters know that they have a need for the new practice. They are not interested in changing for the sake of change, like an innovator. They will listen to reason and will apply new solutions pragmatically.

Early Majority: This group is typically larger, usually approximately one third of the population adopting the practice. This group needs evidence from the first two groups before attempting the idea. Change is not seen as a priority, either because the current practices are comfortable or because there is no perceived problem to solve.

Late Majority: This group consists of skeptics who resist change. There may be considerable mistrust regarding the motive for the change, or resentment built up from previous changes that have failed.

Laggards: Laggards are people who would rather resign or be fired than change how they work. They see no point in changing because their problems are perceived as un-

---

1. You may also want to read [Peters85] and [Moore91]. These books present the adoption curve with different degrees of detail. [Rogers62] is the oldest and most detailed.

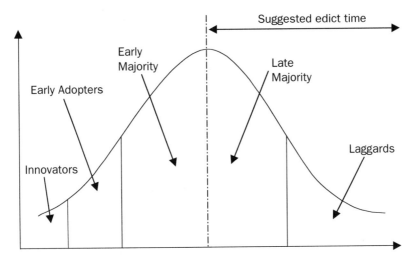

Figure 2–1   The adoption curve.

solvable, or the current practices appear to work fine. A laggard knows that a paycheck will arrive in the mail regardless of whether the change occurs.

Each of your customers can be placed in one of the categories by assessing his receptiveness to the proposed change. Use the adoption curve to help determine who needs which solution, when they need it, and whom to avoid until the majority of the people have adopted the new practice.

Using the Adoption Curve

You can use the adoption curve in three ways when deploying a change:

1. Increase the speed of deployment by determining with whom to work and in which order.

2. Reduce the risk of failure by building and deploying the solution in increments. Innovators and early adopters can

provide specific requirements for and feedback on early versions of the solution.

3. Determine when to develop a policy and issue an edict.

Increase the Speed of Deployment

Always target the innovators and early adopters first. They have a willingness and need to try the new idea. If you pick people in the beginning who are unwilling to try something new or don't see any need to change, all you will prove is that they are indeed unwilling and have no need!

When you work with innovators, be aware that they are usually perceived as fanatics or a fringe element. People who consider themselves *normal* tend to reject the opinions of the fringe as impractical. Work with the innovators to test new ideas and concepts. The innovators will derive benefit from your solution, and you will gain experience that can be used when you work with the early adopters.

The early adopters are your greatest allies. Focus on their needs and problems and use selected examples from the innovators, taking special care to focus on practical demonstrations of how the new idea has improved things. Show them specifically how the idea can be applied to meet their needs. In addition to the innovators, early adopters will help you get started, try new practices, and help you improve any inadequacies in the solution you are advocating. The solution you provide to the remaining groups will be better tested and more robust. Success stories from this group can be used to influence the others.

The members of the early majority are careful and deliberate in their adoption of new practices. They may need evidence that the new practices are effective and are being used successfully by the other people. They also take more time in deciding to adopt any new idea. Because this group is large, there will be varying levels of resistance. Be patient with the early majority; many of them will prefer to watch others try things and see the results.

Your earlier successes with innovators and early adopters may cause you to assume that working with the early majority will be as easy. On the contrary. Assume that the early majority will require more coaching and selling to get them to adopt the practices that others have tried. Deployment of new practices often dies right here [Moore91].

When you work with the late majority, focus on their needs also. Provide ample success stories to help them see that others are using the ideas and have proved their utility. It is especially helpful to use the opinion leaders, usually early adopters, to help sway them. Nothing is quite as effective as a good demonstration of the practices in use. It is unlikely that they will rush to the new idea; instead, they will want to see other people putting it to good use. Some members of this group will continually think up reasons why your solution will not work and try to change your focus. By the time you work with the late majority, be sure you have solid support from managers for each practice. Managers can help reinforce these practices and encourage adoption.

As for the laggards, in the beginning, ignore them. Certainly, visit them to understand their concerns and address them if you can; however, don't waste too much time trying to convert the unconvertible. By the time the late majority have adopted the solution, either the evidence so far will have converted them, or they might comply, albeit superficially, under an edict. If you were to work with the most difficult group first, not only would you encounter resistance, but you would also increase the likelihood of failure stories spreading across the organization. Bad news travels quickly.

The laggards usually have to sink lower in their day-to-day problems before they are willing to change. They have to feel pain. Make them aware of successes experienced by other groups in the organization and talk to their managers about how others have solved these problems. If you can't wait for them to develop a need for what you have, certainly consider making the solution an edict. However, keep in mind that laggards can perform any new practice academically and still not realize the results for which you are hoping.

When you work with a laggard, curb your enthusiasm. Be helpful, calm, and matter-of-fact. Enthusiasm can make your claims sound untested and unrealistic. Address obstacles that may send them running. Laggards are always on the lookout for evidence that supports their initial belief that the change is unworkable and academic. Help them adopt new practices in small, useful pieces.

Reduce the Risk of Failure

If your solution is complex, you may want to consider breaking it up into components. The audience you have in mind for the complete solution will probably not need every component immediately. For example, if you are developing a planning process, you may have components for estimation, risk management, negotiation, status reviews, and approvals. Identify the components that the innovators and early adopters need and develop them first. Use the feedback from your first users to design and refine the next increment.

Some of the managers will be innovators and early adopters for the negotiation piece, whereas some of the developers will be innovators and early adopters for the estimation piece. As you progress through your customer base to "sell" your solutions to others, revisit your initial innovators and early adopters, because they may now be ready for the next increment. With this approach, you will build your complete planning solution in the order it is needed and experience early progress for the pieces that are complete.

In one company, the software developers were planning to implement an audit program to verify execution of their software life cycle. Auditing the complete life cycle was an overwhelming task, and proposing the idea generated many skeptics and laggards. There were no innovators or early adopters for the complete solution. When we asked the developers for two or three essential areas that needed verifying, they identified early adopters for small pieces of the audit process. They also identified three critical areas that would benefit from being checked for correctness using the audit process. These areas were creating CD releases, making commitments to a customer, and resolving defects. We addressed these activities first.

Determine When to Develop a Policy and Issue an Edict

Many improvement teams develop policy statements at the start of their improvement activity. A policy states under what circumstances a practice will be used. For example, a risk management policy might state that the risk management process should be used on projects that cost more than $50,000. When first developing a risk management process, it may be difficult to predict all the conditions during which the practice would be most beneficial. It is much easier to develop a policy after some experience has been gained using the solution. One option is to delay the development of the policy statement until the early majority has experience using the process.

You can use pilot projects to ensure that policy statements are well written and appropriate. Many people successfully pilot tools and processes but then try to develop an organizationwide policy stating that the tool or process should be adopted immediately. In such cases, the policy could be full of errors and may lead to misunderstandings about when the tool or process must be used. Instead, pilot the policy itself and determine its readiness for wide-scale use.

In one company, the vice president decided that a scheduling tool would be helpful to address planning and scheduling problems. After six months of tool evaluation, the company selected a scheduling tool and simultaneously issued a policy stating that all projects were expected to use the tool by the end of the year. The policy statement did not adequately take into account the difference between large and small projects. It also did not recognize that each project team might have other more pressing planning problems to fix. Trying the policy on a limited set of pilot projects would have helped the company determine when the tool was necessary.

Requiring universal adoption of a solution is usually premature when only the innovators and early adopters have tried it. Such broad edicts can generate resistance and delay widespread adoption of a new practice. A good time to issue an edict is when approximately 50 percent of the organization is using the solution effectively. At the 50 percent point, the success stories can be used to influence the late majority and laggards. It will be difficult, but not impossible, for them to resist in the face of such evidence. At 50 percent, there is no majority opposing the idea.

You may decide to use an edict earlier if the consequences of not using the solution could lead to a negative business impact. You could even stagger the deployment of an edict. One organization decided that all system interface descriptions should go through a formal peer review, while delaying the decision to require peer reviews on other aspects of the system until the organization gained more peer review experience.

Overcoming Resistance

Resistance has two common causes: First, it is not apparent to the person resisting that your solution will meet his current needs. Second, the person believes that your solution brings more pain than benefit. Examples of pain include embarrassment (if the change is unsuccessful), wasted time using a poorly constructed solution, and fear of stepping into the unknown (when the status quo is comfortable).

You can address the first common cause by identifying and clarifying the needs of your audience. What is the problem and what are they trying to accomplish? Do they understand your proposed solution and is this an appropriate time to adopt the idea? What are their concerns regarding costs? If your solution does not match the need, then say so, and investigate other solutions that do. If the issue is timing or cost, determine a more appropriate occasion to deploy the new skill, or propose a smaller, more economical solution. If you conclude that your solution matches the need but you are still unable to make any progress, consider the second common cause of resistance: the belief that the change will be too painful.

Beliefs held by the individual drive the resistance you are experiencing. These beliefs are based on the person's current knowledge and previous experiences with similar issues. Your task is to understand his current beliefs about the solution you are proposing.

For example, one quality assurance person was adamantly against peer reviews—a technique used to find defects in documents and code. This individual certainly had a need for finding defects, because that was part of his daily job. In his experience, however, peer reviews were team sessions used to point fingers at the document author, and the resulting document was degraded by the inputs. Based on this experience, he believed that peer reviews were just another "design-by-committee" approach.

Resistance was overcome by demonstrating a well-run peer review. This time, critical defects were found. The peer review provided constructive, impersonal feedback that significantly improved the final document. This experience changed his belief about peer reviews.

Determine beliefs by asking, "What experiences do you have with X?" or "What have you heard about X from others?" Once you understand someone's beliefs, you may decide that they are sound and appropriate, and that your solution, in hindsight, is inappropriate. If you can offer better information to correct a false belief, constructively offer it. Then go the extra mile and demonstrate how your solution does indeed help.

When you encounter resistance, verify that the people resisting are indeed the correct target audience. If you approach a group of individuals that does not need the solution you are advocating, they might be resisting for a good reason. The group might not be able to articulate the fact that they are not your correct audience.

In one company, the improvement team was developing processes for subcontract management. The people resisting initially sounded like laggards. After further discussion, it became apparent that there were different audiences for each part of the process. The process for selecting subcontractors had a different audience than the process for tracking subcontractor performance. High-level managers selected subcontractors and project leads tracked them throughout project implementation. The subcontract management process was therefore broken into components, and each component was developed and refined using a different audience.

In another company, we taught our project planning class to several project managers who resisted all of our techniques. We initially suspected that they were all laggards, until we asked for clarification on what their "project manager" job entailed. Then we realized that we had the wrong audience. For them, project management meant managing customer relationships, not running the internal workings of a software project.

No Time for Adoption Curves?

You may feel that using the adoption curve to identify and work with innovators and early adopters first is too slow an approach for your organization. If your goal is to adopt 120 new practices from the action plan during the next six months, you might wonder if you are going to come close to this goal. Remember that many organizations that rush adoption do not actually adopt the practices in the long term. If you ask the developers and managers what they actually do, you will find that some practices are being used well, some superficially, but many are not used at all. People cannot master and internalize a new technique in a single day, but they can certainly pretend!

Ignoring the adoption curve can delay the deployment of new ideas. The more resistance you encounter by working with the wrong people, the longer deployment will take. Progress is quicker with the innovators and early adopters because their resistance is minimal. Early success stories can motivate the skeptics into action and provide you with experience of the solution before working with less enthusiastic groups.

If your organization has numerous problems, fire fighting may be so chronic that it allows no time for even innovators and early adopters to take action. In this situation, consider dividing the proposed improvement into smaller, more manageable pieces. For example, if a team wanted to improve configuration management, select the most relevant piece to the team's current project goal. Choose a small piece that can be applied in one half day or less, so the team members have a chance to squeeze it into their busy schedule.

One project team often sent incorrect files to the test group. Believing they did not have time to work on configuration management, the team allowed this problem to continue. The improvement team proposed allocating two hours before the next test phase to construct a list stating the correct files for the release. This list was used in subsequent work to prevent the problem from occurring again.

When you work with a team that is always in crisis, provide support to reduce the overhead of the improvement. Schedule rooms, call out for pizza, buy snacks, and facilitate the session. Over the long term, allow the team to perform these tasks by themselves to become self-sufficient. If you need to, take the team off-site to avoid interruption. A coffee shop is almost free and is usually away from colleagues and e-mail.

Accelerating Adoption Through Training and Consulting
You can accelerate adoption by working with adopters in parallel, using a larger number of knowledgeable staff to provide the expertise. Process champions—individuals who have a strong interest in promoting a new practice—can be especially helpful for both generating interest and helping with training. For example, if you have developed a risk management process, you could teach this to champions who then teach it to others in their organizations. Each manager could identify someone in his organization to be trained to teach the method internally.

The most effective choice for a trainer is someone who is highly respected and has the skills to share information with others. Use credible champions to help ensure that students pay attention. People adopt new skills faster when a credible source conveys the material in a manner perceived as useful. Careful selection of teachers significantly impacts both speed of adoption and application of the skill.

At one company, we trained a senior manager to teach a three-day project planning class. He then taught classes to his developers and project managers. Because the message came from a credible source, students were quick to adopt the new practices. Similarly, a senior software manager in a large defense contract organization taught software inspection to her developers. Because the message came from this person and because she used inspections for her own work, engineers took it seriously.

Any train-the-trainer implementation runs the risk of conveying a message different from the one intended. Reduce this risk by spending time with the trainer to observe his teaching ability and to verify adequate understanding of the subject. Keep the message accurate and consistent by providing the trainer with thorough teaching materials, including a version of the slides with teaching tips for the trainer.

When process champions are used as trainers, make the solutions they teach relatively small and self-contained. This helps keep the deployment program simple. Examples include four-hour presentations on risk, inspection, unit test, system test, estimation, scheduling techniques, project postmortems, or the use of a scheduling tool. Hands-on workshops, during which real problems are discussed and possible solutions are developed, are particularly effective. More detailed classes may be needed, but most process champions do not have the time to develop or teach these classes.

When choosing between developing training materials in-house and purchasing training from vendors, consider your current internal expertise and ability to sustain the effort with internal people. Often you will want to use something that already exists or can be tailored to meet your needs. Ideas that have been around for a long time and have readily available training should usually be purchased from outside. Topics specific to your business may need to be developed from scratch. First look at what is available, how closely it meets your needs, costs based on instructor rates, copyright constraints and license fees, and then decide to tailor it or create your own version. It may not be cost-effective to reinvent what has already been done well before.

Process champions already have full-time jobs that limit their availability as instructors. We have seen many examples when companies have adopted the train-the-trainer approach and, after two months, the trainers were reassigned to other unrelated full-time positions. If you use champions, obtain an agreement about their availability. Unless they can spend a significant time training each month for six months, you will spend much of your time training new trainers.

In parallel with training, consider more intensive consulting to help your organization adopt new techniques.

If you are reading this book as an in-house consultant, 40 to 60 percent of your time will probably be spent on helping teams adopt new practices. You can begin by following the ideas presented in Chapter 1. Start with understanding one project team's needs, and then help identify and apply solutions.

For example, if a project needs help estimating development schedules, learn a technique, facilitate a project estimation session, and see how it well it works. Facilitated sessions work especially well because you can combine teaching and hands-on work using their actual project. When you have led a few sessions, you can teach the team how to conduct sessions without you.

Consultation and facilitation work because you are there to make sure that each new practice is tried correctly. You can debrief with the team to determine how the technique could be modified to meet their needs better. For further education on consulting skills, we recommend that you read, *The Secret of Consulting* by Weinberg [Weinberg85] and *Flawless Consulting* by Peter Block [Block99].

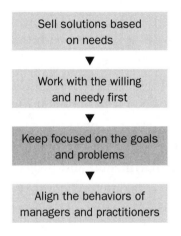

KEEP FOCUSED ON THE GOALS AND PROBLEMS

Improvement programs always begin with the best intentions. Often, however, the focus becomes diluted and ineffective, with many tangential issues entering the picture. You can maintain focus by keeping the goals and problems firmly in the minds of the target audience. The plan you developed in Chapter 1 should be your primary guide.

One software company identified a clear need for better project planning during its process assessment. Consensus was achieved among 60 people and planning became a compelling issue to fix. Two months later, an internal document recommended the development of a project-planning database. Project managers were to use historical data from this database to improve their estimates. At this point, the job of developing the database became the purpose of the improvement effort. The project-planning problem, carefully worded during the assessment, was out of sight and out of mind. Three years later, the organization had a database containing almost no usable data, and their project-planning problem remained unsolved. If the people involved in the improvement effort had kept the clear statement of the project-planning problem as their focus, they might have recognized that their efforts were not fixing the problem.

It is easy to focus on improvement activities but lose sight of the intended result. For example, teams using the SEI CMM often become focused on the Key Process Areas and documentation. Organizations using ISO9001 often become focused on creating procedures and collecting records. Rather than allowing the improvement activities to become the goal, regularly revisit your plan and keep your actions in alignment with the original goals and problems. When you discover a mismatch, update the improvement plan or redirect your group's actions to support the true goal. Continue to use the elements from the framework to support your plan.

One way to keep goals and problems visible is to review improvement plans periodically during departmental and project meetings. If you are not making weekly gains in your improvement program, you may be offtrack. Weekly gains come from fixing numerous, small project-level problems.

By keeping appropriate attention focused on your goals and problems, you can avoid one of the most common pitfalls: wasting your efforts on activities that are unimportant to your organization.

Doing Too Much at Once

When you have motivating goals and problems in your action plan, it is tempting to try to do too many things at once. Rushing improvements and creating ineffective solutions can cause frustration and burnout. Success in any discipline is accomplished by focusing on a few items at a time. Stick to the priorities you established in your plan and move sequentially through the actions. See a few improvements to completion so the organization can experience success. Early successes provide fuel and motivation to address remaining goals and problems.

Sell solutions based
on needs

▼

Work with the willing
and needy first

▼

Keep focused on the goals
and problems

▼

Align the behaviors of
managers and practitioners

ALIGN THE BEHAVIORS OF MANAGERS AND PRACTITIONERS

Without effective leadership, good improvement efforts usually derail. Managers can help keep the efforts on track by providing a clear focus for each improvement, letting people know what is expected of them, and aligning their own behavior with the improvement.

Managers need to ensure that the organization stays focused on its business goals and related improvements. Too often, people get sidetracked from their improvement effort because they are too busy, or they don't see the relevance of current improvement tasks to their work.

To help an organization stay focused, managers must remain informed about the planned improvements and help people see how the new practices support organizational goals. For example, if meeting product delivery deadlines is most important, ensure that individuals understand how current improvements, such as risk management and scheduling, address that goal.

For each new practice, a manager needs to understand

- ◆ What the practice is supposed to accomplish (that is, what problem it is fixing or what goal it is supporting)
- ◆ How and when the practice should be used
- ◆ How he can ensure its success

Managers will then need to communicate this information to their people. For example, an introduction to a new estimation process should describe its purpose, why it is needed, and how it should be used. A manager should explain how the estimation process can estimate any kind of project, provide a detailed task list, clarify project assumptions, and build consensus among the project members. He could also say that it is needed to help meet current deadlines, scope the project correctly, increase schedule predictability, and reduce cost overruns.

When advocating a new estimation process, managers can use several strategies to help make it successful. They can require project teams to prepare estimates before performing project work. They can provide time in the current schedule to perform the estimation process and require the recording of estimates to build a historical database.

Managers must change their behavior to support the new practices. If people see a manager using the new method or consistently asking for the results of the new method, they know the manager is serious. A vice president who plans her work using the standard planning process sends a strong message about the vital nature of the improvement effort and the method's usefulness. To lead by example, managers can use the new risk management process for their own work, use the new inspection or peer review process to inspect their documents, use a tailored version of the new requirements elicitation method to understand the requirements of developers and other managers, and demonstrate the use of appropriate metrics.

Aligning management and practitioner behaviors also requires a review of your current reward system. Managers usually get what they reward. For example, rewarding participation in planning encourages smooth-running projects with fewer surprises. Rewarding bug fixing and emergency patches encourages the premature release of products and increased rework. Reinforce the improvement program by rewarding improvements that lead to the desired results. Avoid rewarding activities that don't reflect the group's long-term goals.

SUMMARY

Deploying numerous practices across an organization can be overwhelming. You can streamline deployment by selecting an appropriate time and place for each improvement. Understanding who needs which improvement and when they need it can help you *pull* the practices into the organization and avoid resistance.

Sales skills enable you to understand the needs of your audience and the time frame for servicing each need. The adoption curve enables you to identify groups of people who want to change now and other groups that do not.

To enable sustained progress, build solutions in small pieces, focus on specific audiences, and align the behaviors of managers and practitioners.

Quick Start

- Interview several project teams and make notes on which project members are the innovators and early adopters, and what they are ready to adopt. Also, note the late majority (skeptics) and laggards. Refine your current improvement action plan using this information.

- Deploy solutions in small pieces based on project needs and priorities. For example, a complete project planning process can be broken into estimation, negotiation, risk identification, and scheduling.

- Interview some managers and find one who can use some of the techniques you are advocating, such as estimating, planning, or peer reviews.

- Identify someone who can help deploy well-tried improvements in parallel with your efforts.

3
Checking Progress

"You can design a measurement system for
any conclusion you wish to draw."
—Gerald Weinberg, *Quality Software Management*
[Weinberg97]

This chapter discusses how to track the progress of your improvement program and take corrective action. Tracking progress lets you know how well your improvement program is going, provides visibility to detect problems early, and gives you data to make your future plans more effective. Corrective action consists of mid-course changes based on results and lessons learned from the *planning and implementation* phases. Corrective actions include revising an action plan to achieve an unattained goal, revising the planning approach used during the planning phase, changing how new skills are developed and deployed during the implementation phase, realigning the improvement program with new priorities, or revising the metrics used to monitor progress.

In this chapter we provide examples of how companies track improvement and take corrective actions. Tailor these examples to fit your needs or use them as a starting point to generate your own tracking and corrective action ideas.[1]

Four questions can help your organization examine how well the improvement program is going:

1. Are we making progress on the goals?
2. Are we making progress on our improvement plan?
3. Are we making progress on the improvement framework?
4. What lessons have we learned so far?

ARE WE MAKING PROGRESS ON THE GOALS?

In Chapter 1, business goals drove the development of the action plan during the planning stage. The GQM approach was used to derive metrics that provided feedback on whether these business goals were achieved. Table 3–1 presents an example of this approach from Chapter 1. Checking progress toward completion of each goal helps you see how effective your improvement effort has been to date.

The following tracking examples illustrate some of the metrics listed in Table 3–1. For each metric described, we also discuss corrective actions taken by the organization based on the data.

---

1. When you are ready for more detailed information on metrics, look at [Yanamura97] *Practical Software Metrics for Project Management and Process Improvement* and *Successful Software Process Improvement* by Robert Grady [Grady92, Grady97].

Table 3–1 The GQM Approach to Defining Metrics

Goal	Questions	Metrics
Meet all our cost and schedule commitments.	Are we spending the planned number of hours on the project to complete it? Are we hitting our milestones?	Planned versus actual effort for each project. The number of days each milestone is early or late
Deliver product X by mm/dd/yy.	Are we spending the planned number of hours on the project to complete it? Are we hitting our milestones?	Planned versus actual effort for each project milestone. The number of days each milestone is early or late
Reduce rework to less than 20 percent of total project effort.	How much time do we spend on rework now? How does this compare with our development time and are we improving?	Percentage of project time spent on rework
	How many defects do we have in the product during design and coding?	Defect density: number of defects found per unit size of work product (for example, number of pages of design, number of lines of code)
Improve the performance of our core software product. (Target to be defined.)	What is our current performance?	Average screen response time during peak system usage
Achieve customer rating of 9/10 on product evaluation form.	How satisfied are they now? Are we improving?	Annual customer satisfaction survey
Keep profits at 15 percent (and costs at the same level as last year).	What is our profit? Is it getting better or worse?	Annual net profit

Goal: Meet All Our Cost and Schedule Commitments

Two metrics tracked progress for this goal:

1. A comparison of the planned versus actual effort required to complete each project

2. The number of days each milestone was early or late

Sample Metric: Planned Versus Actual Effort for Each Project

One of the lines of business for this organization was selling customized versions of its core product line. Each custom change was treated as a separate project. Tracking estimated and actual costs ensured that they were correctly charging for each change. They tracked costs by comparing estimated labor hours with actual hours expended on each project (Figure 3–1). At the end

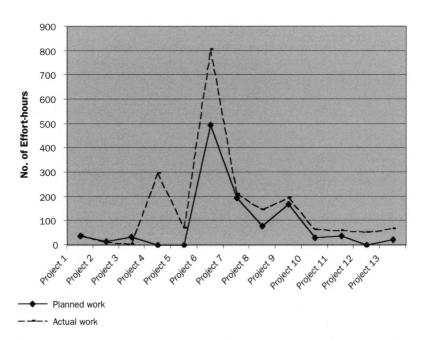

Figure 3–1   Planned versus actual effort-hours required to complete each project.

of each project, they analyzed the differences in the total number of actual hours spent versus the original estimate. They incorporated lessons learned into the next estimation cycle.

Tracking the data for each custom project showed a trend of consistently underestimating the number of hours needed. Although the group met the majority of their deadlines, the hours expended to do so were causing some financial loss. The group refined the estimation process by developing a spreadsheet of this historical information and using it when estimating new projects. They also shared the data with the sales staff to develop a joint understanding of how to bid on future change requests.

Sample Metric: The Number of Days Each Milestone Is Early or Late

The organization also tracked milestone completion for the phases of each project, in addition to monitoring overall cost commitments. By observing the differences in planned and actual milestone completion dates, each team improved its ability to predict whether the final date would be met. The organization constructed a graph, similar to the one in Figure 3–2, for each project. This allowed project members to see which milestones were being missed and by how much. It was also clear which phases had the most problems and where scheduling improvements needed to be made.

In this example, the primary problem was late completion of the *Programming finalized* milestone. This delay did not affect completion of the test plan, but it did impact verification and final testing. Based on this data and similar observations of other projects, the team took corrective actions. They started using historical data to estimate future programming phases and began factoring the dependency between development and testing into the project's formal schedule.

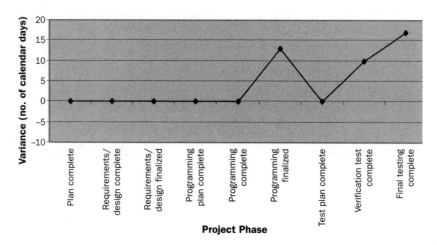

Figure 3–2   Variances in the schedule performance for one project.

The metric shown in Figure 3–2 is good for tracking project progress. It informs the project which downstream milestones are likely to encounter problems based on earlier delays. The weakness of this metric is that the deadline problem is not known until it actually occurs. To address this issue, the team planned on adopting a measurement concept called *earned value*, which tracks task completion in parallel with effort expenditure. Earned value data indicates situations when a task is not complete but the effort budgeted for the task has already been expended. Because earned value highlights the milestone completion problem earlier, it provides a longer lead time for corrective action. To learn more about earned value, read *A Discipline in Software Engineering*, by Watts Humphrey [Humphrey95].

Goal: Reduce Rework to Less Than 20 Percent of Total Project Effort

When organizations embark on an improvement program, reducing rework is a common starting point. The time spent in

rework activities (such as analyzing defects, deciding which defects to fix, fixing them, and retesting) can often consume significant resources. This time is mostly eliminated when a project
adopts sound software engineering practices. In the following
two examples, teams tracked reduction in rework in two ways.
They examined the amount of time spent performing rework
activities versus new development, and they tracked the number
of defects found in source code.

Sample Metric: Percentage of Project Time Spent in Rework
In this example, the software development group tracked the
percentage of its time spent fixing defects (Figure 3-3). This data
communicated the impact of the improvement program in a
meaningful way to the organization's management team.

At the beginning of their improvement program, rework rep-
resented 45 percent of the project's total effort. After five
months of improvement, rework claimed 33 percent. The improvements made during this period were focused on effort estimation, risk management, schedule creation, project tracking,
and inspection of design documents. After one year, time spent

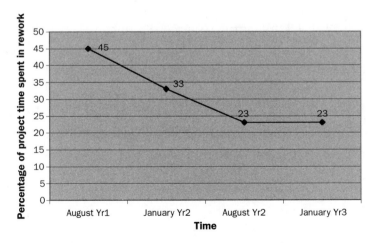

Figure 3–3   Percentage of project time spent in rework.

on rework dropped to 23 percent. Between January of year 2 and August of the same year, improvements included inspecting code and requirements documents, formal configuration management, improved testing, process assurance, and conducting postproject sessions on lessons learned.

The last two data points in the graph show that one hour of rework was spent for every 3.4 hours of development (23 percent of the project's total effort). The graph remained static between August of year 2 and January of year 3 as they refined their current practices. The improvement plan at the beginning of year 3 included adopting use cases [Wiegers99] to reduce requirements-related defects and employing a design process to reduce design-related defects. These planned improvements were expected to move the organization to its 20 percent goal. No further corrective action was necessary.[2]

Sample Metric: Defect Density

You can also track reductions in rework by measuring the defect density of work products developed by the project team. In the following examples, two organizations measured defect density for code. Defects were identified using an inspection (peer review) technique.

The data in Figure 3–4 is from an organization just embarking on its improvement journey. It shows the number of defects (severity 1 and severity 2) found in seven code modules selected from the company's product suite. Some modules had already been released to customers; the remainder had been through unit testing and were about to enter system testing. Each module underwent inspection by a team of five people. The inspection data established a baseline picture of the current rework

---

2. For additional reading on the benefits of reducing rework, see [Dion93].

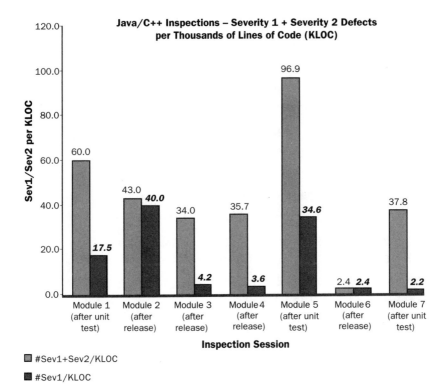

Figure 3–4   Establishing a baseline metric to understand the current rework problem.[3]

problem, where approximately 70 percent of each developer's time was spent rewriting code that did not work.

From this small amount of data, it was obvious that code after unit test and code released to the field was very poor. These defects, and ones similar to these in other areas of their code base, were the primary source of their rework problem. The organization started corrective action by using the inspection technique on other critical areas of code. They only selected a few additional areas initially, because their current project

---

3. The results of seven inspected code modules were measured in defects per thousands of lines of code (KLOC).

schedules did not allow much time for removing defects before release, even though they found time for significant rework activities after release.

Further analysis of the data showed that many defects were situations when the program did not check for invalid input such as empty data structures and null pointers. Investigation showed that the code sample labeled "Module 6 (after release)" had few defects because the author had built-in checks for incoming defective data. From these observations, the team created a checklist to remind developers of these programming practices.

Figure 3–5 shows data for a different organization that had a similar rework improvement goal. This organization had been assessed at SEI CMM Level 4 and had been working aggressively on improvement for seven years. The data shows that, on average, inspection revealed 1.3 defects per 100 physical lines of

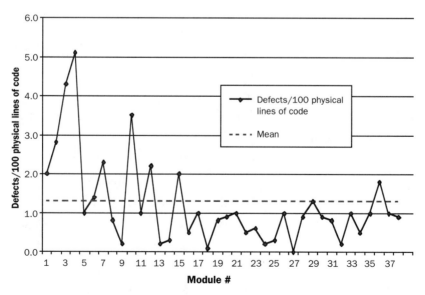

Figure 3–5   Defect density for code modules in one project.

code.[4] The system test phase, performed after the code had been inspected and reworked, found an average of 0.14 defects per 100 physical lines of code. With fewer defects reaching the end user, postrelease project rework was negligible.

Analysis determined that code defect density was improving; therefore, no specific corrective action was taken. To maintain its desired rework reduction goal, the group continued inspecting its code base and other work products for errors.[5]

ARE WE MAKING PROGRESS ON OUR IMPROVEMENT PLAN?

The major milestones in the improvement plan are the goals and intermediate goals established during the planning phase. An organization makes progress when it achieves these goals. This is analogous to tracking milestone completion within a software project. You can check off goals and actions on the plan, or use a trend chart to show the rate of progress.

Deciding on whether an intermediate goal is complete can be a judgment call. One definition of "complete" is that the problem described by the intermediate goal no longer exists to any noticeable degree and no further work is needed on this issue. This definition may highlight that one part of the organization has solved the problem but not another. If so, add a section to your plan to solve the problem in the remaining parts of the organization and list the actions required to accomplish this.

---

4. This equates to 13 defects per KLOC compared with the previous example in Figure 3–4, which averaged 44 defects per KLOC.

5. See [Florac99] for further examples of metric interpretation techniques.

In Figure 3–6, one organization tracked progress for 11 goals contained within their plan. By month 8, we can see that the improvement plan is unlikely to be completed by the desired deadline of 16 months. In this example, corrective action consisted of revising the completion date to 24 months, based on current performance. This was the organization's first attempt at improvement and the team realized that the original plan was too aggressive based on their current project workload.

Alternative options for corrective action include dedicating more time for improvement, using success stories from the early adopters to motivate skeptics, and ensuring that you are not developing solutions that already exist elsewhere.

ARE WE MAKING PROGRESS ON THE IMPROVEMENT FRAMEWORK?

If you have adopted an improvement framework, you will need a method of checking your progress. Most improvement frameworks have a formal assessment or audit mechanism available to monitor their adoption, (such as the appraisal methods for CMM and CMM Integration [CMMI] [Dunaway96, SCAMPI00]); however, these mechanisms can take several days to perform and are not always a practical choice for frequent intermediate progress checks. Two faster, but less thorough, alternatives for checking progress include counting the actions completed in the action plan that came from the framework and performing a check called a *mini-assessment* [Sakry93].

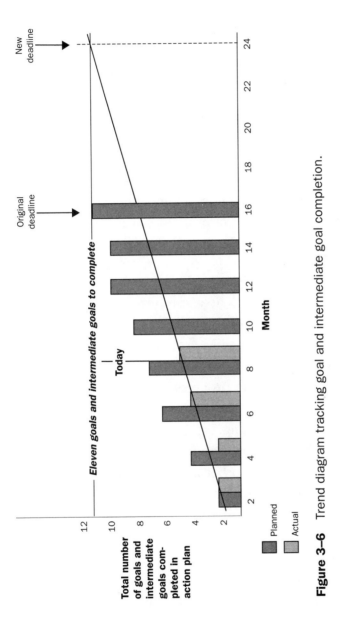

Figure 3–6 Trend diagram tracking goal and intermediate goal completion.

Counting the Completed Actions

You can check progress on adopting elements of an improvement framework by determining which elements from the framework are complete. Counting these actions as a percentage of all the elements required for the improvement framework provides an indicator of progress.

In the example shown in Figure 3–7, five actions in the plan are complete, as indicated by checkmarks in the *Status* column. Three are CMM Level 2 activities. Completing this part of the action plan resulted in 2 percent progress toward CMM Level 2.

Mini-Assessment

Another method of tracking an organization's progress against an improvement framework is a mini-assessment [Sakry93, Carr00]. A mini-assessment obtains a quick snapshot of your improvement program. A mini-assessment is not an audit [Jalote00, Humphrey89] or a full process assessment, but rather a small check to determine progress. Results from the mini-assessment indicate how fast improvement is taking place so you can detect any backsliding.

A mini-assessment is a process-focused, not a goal-focused, progress check. Therefore, other goal-oriented metrics should accompany it so the mini-assessment is not the sole means of determining progress. When a process check is the sole measure of progress, it is easy for an organization to lose sight of the overall purpose of the improvement program and become overly focused on the process score. By adding business-oriented metrics such as product end user satisfaction and schedule predictability, an organization can balance metrics that track framework adoption with metrics that reflect business success.

There are seven steps to the mini-assessment process:

1. Plan the assessment.

Action Plan Owner: Jane

Primary Goal and Intermediate Goals (The results you want)	Purpose of Goal (Why do you want to achieve the goal?)	Actions	Priority (*essential)	Time Estimate	Who	Status
Reduce product development cycle to six to nine months for product X	Deliver earlier than competition					
Manage changing requirements (based on problem 1).	Prevent schedule slips resulting from expensive scope changes.	Only allow changes to the application interface, not to the kernel routines.	1*	4 hrs	Jane	√
		Establish a group with the authority for managing the project's software baselines.	2*	4 hrs	Pradeep	√
		Check progress and take corrective action.[6]	—	2 hrs	Jane	√

continued

6. This is a placeholder for the activities described in this chapter.

Figure 3–7   Counting the actions in the action plan that are from the improvement framework.

Primary Goal and Intermediate Goals (The results you want)	Purpose of Goal (Why do you want to achieve the goal?)	Actions	Priority (*essential)	Time Estimate	Who	Status
		Improve the library control system to minimize version control errors. Investigate requirements management tools.	3	80 hrs	Fred	√
	Elements from CMM Level 2	Record and track change requests and problem reports for all configuration items.	4	2 hrs/week	Jane	√
		Review the initial requirements and changes before they are incorporated into the project plan.	5	2 hrs/week	Mike	√
		Baseline the requirements before design commences.	6	20 hrs	Jane	

Figure 3-7 Counting the actions in the action plan that are from the improvement framework (continued).

2. Meet with the interviewees to explain what will be checked and how.

3. Perform the mini-assessment interview.

4. Communicate the results.

5. Debrief the mini-assessment process.

6. Improve the questionnaire.

7. Take corrective action.

Here we discuss the primary results and sample corrective actions taken. Appendix F describes the complete mini-assessment process in detail.

Before conducting a mini-assessment, decide which practices you will check for adoption. These could include activities described by the organization's development life cycle, CMM, ISO9001, or another improvement framework. Develop a list of questions based on these criteria, typically one question for each practice. You can also include additional questions to verify that problems identified during previous assessments have been addressed. In the example in Figure 3–8, the last question checks to see whether a previously identified network problem has been fixed.

Sample mini-assessment questions

Describe how your team

- Performs inspections or walkthroughs for key work products (such as code, design, test cases, and test plans)
- Performs black-box testing
- Performs white-box testing
- Performs version control of all significant work products (from plans to code)

Do you have adequate computer network stability (compared with the problem reported in the last assessment)?

Figure 3–8 Example of criteria for the mini-assessment.

The first result of the mini-assessment is a summary of the strengths and areas for improvement for the project being assessed. During the mini-assessment process, the assessment team takes note of practices that are performed well and areas that need improvement. These notes are summarized and presented to the project at a followup communication session. An example is shown in Figure 3–9.

The second result of the mini-assessment is the number of favorable responses from the mini-assessment questions. The assessment team calculates the percentage of favorable responses and communicates it back to each project. At the end of the communication session, the project members can select a few areas for the next improvement phase and revise its improvement plan.

A bar chart indicating the overall percent of favorable responses graphically communicates the average project score for all projects assessed. The sample charts in Figures 3–10 and 3–11 show the trends of each group. If the organization is very

---

Project A: Strengths and areas for improvement

Strengths

- Inspections are performed on requirements and code.
- Black-box testing is performed against the requirements.
- White-box testing is performed on critical code.
- Work products are under configuration management (in other words, project plans, requirements, code, test plans, and test cases).

Areas for improvement

- Computer network stability has not changed since it was reported in the last assessment.
- Project plans for projects larger than three months would benefit from inspection.
- Test plans would benefit from inspection to reduce the amount of redundancy in the test approach.

Figure 3–9   A small example of mini-assessment results for one project.

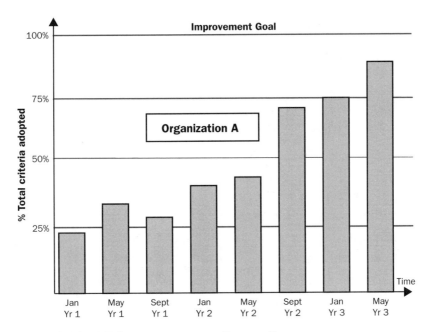

Figure 3–10 Mini-assessment results over time.

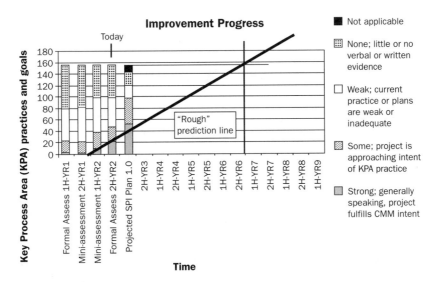

Figure 3–11 Graph from mini-assessment data showing improvement progress (overall company average).

large, you may decide to communicate the results separately for each major division.

In the example in Figure 3–10, the organization performed mini-assessments every four months. The data indicates that during the first year, organization A made progress between January and May and lost ground in September. Attrition of personnel caused this decline. During the early stages of an improvement program, a few people drive the practices of the organization. If these people leave, the practices can leave too.

In Figure 3–11, another organization tabulated its mini-assessment data to show progress toward achieving CMM Level 2, broken down into 154 individual elements. They categorized responses to show partial satisfaction of the CMM components. Response categories were

- Not applicable
- None; little or no verbal or written evidence
- Weak; current practice or plans are weak or inadequate
- Some; project is approaching intent of key process area practice
- Strong; generally speaking, project fulfills CMM intent

The rough prediction line on the graph shows that all 154 elements might be complete by the second half of year 6 based on actual progress since the first half of year 2. The action plan (see "Projected SPI Plan 1.0" in Figure 3–11), developed for the first half of year 3, predicts that more elements will be adopted within the next six months. The rough prediction line is an early warning to the organization. Its precision is not important in this example. It is clear that the original target date for CMM Level 2, which was the first half of year 4, is impossible to meet.

When you track progress, we suggest you keep individual project data in confidence. Each team can obtain data about its own progress for the purpose of its own improvement. The focus of management should be on organizationwide trends.

The last step of the mini-assessment process is taking corrective action based on mini-assessment results. Here we describe examples from two companies.

Example 1: A Company Making Major Improvement Strides

The company depicted in Figure 3–10 produces software for the health care and banking industries. Software engineers are organized into two groups: one group for small customer-driven product changes and one group for developing the company's primary product suite. Their improvement program followed the goal-problem approach described in Chapter 1.

At the end of each organizationwide mini-assessment, the organization determined which problems were still present and the priorities of those problems. These priorities were then fed into a small planning phase to develop a schedule for follow-on improvements. For example, between May and September of year 2, improvements included configuration management and process assurance. Configuration management included establishing a code library, defining a process to manage changes among multiple developers, developing a build process for releases, and tagging defect repairs so that they could be matched with each build. Process assurance included auditing current practices and making suggestions for improvements to the current processes already adopted. Implementing these two significant sets of improvements resulted in the large increase in Figure 3–10.

Many corrective actions included small refinements as the group executed its improvement plan. For example, when a time-tracking tool was installed to track project development activities, the company revised categories of activities numerous times to reflect more accurately the work being performed on each project. When developing a process to manage commitments and share plans between the development and sales staff, they altered the process steps several times to manage new sales commitments and to coordinate various development projects already underway.

This company did not need to take drastic corrective action to keep their improvement program on track. They were self-driven and hooked on self-improvement. All their corrective actions were small, focused on near-term problems, and were tied to project goals.

Example 2: A Company Struggling to Start

The company depicted in Figure 3–11 produces large machines with embedded software. Their organization consists of software engineers split into four groups, each group representing one product line of the company. Six months after their improvement program started, only a few improvements had been made (see "Mini-assessment 2H-YR1" in Figure 3–11).

To evaluate progress, they conducted mini-assessments for each group against a skeleton version of the practices in CMM Level 2. The purpose of each mini-assessment was twofold. First, it determined which CMM practices were being performed on each project. Second, it refocused each team on its improvement activities with a prioritized list of problems. From this data, the improvement team determined how many problems had been resolved compared with the problems listed six months earlier, and how much progress had been made toward the CMM Level 2 criteria.

Analysis of the raw data showed that only one group was making significant progress. The other three groups were too busy fighting fires with product problems. Even though each of these groups agreed that lack of a clear requirements definition and poor tracking of requirements changes were high-priority problems, neither group could find the time to address them. Their lack of motivation to make progress was also striking. This was based on their assumption that senior management didn't care if these problems were solved. If senior management didn't care, why should they?

Charting the mini-assessment data for all groups combined showed that their process maturity goal of CMM Level 2 might be achieved during the second half of year 6 based on current progress. Their target was the first half of year 4. Other business goals such as product shipment and improved customer satisfaction were also in jeopardy.

Corrective action after the mini-assessment was focused on reporting a summary of the mini-assessment data to the chief executive officer and the four division heads. The company needed to take dramatic action to get the improvement program restarted. The primary message in the presentation was that the areas for improvement noted in the mini-assessments were impeding their business goals. The secondary message was that the date for achieving CMM Level 2 would be approximately 30 months later than desired, assuming the current rate of progress. After the meeting, each division head invited the improvement team to its organization to clarify the problems and to help make progress. This step was followed by a planning phase to take another look at the problems and to set new priorities within the group.

In this company, corrective action started with an escalation of the current state of affairs to executive management. Several small corrective actions were also implemented within each project as they tried new practices. These included refining statement-of-work templates to manage third-party vendors, transitioning from a word processor to a tool for managing requirements, and tracking actual hours expended on each project.

Mini-Assessment Summary

The mini-assessment process is an effective way to understand which practices have been adopted and which have not. An organization can use the information to understand current gaps, obtain insight on deployment problems, and provide a basis for replanning the improvement effort. The results of a mini-assessment are secondary measures of progress and should always be accompanied by primary measures based on the goals and problems of the organization.

Measurement Side Effects

When you take measures, behaviors of the people being measured can change inappropriately. Optimizing the measure can become more attractive than fixing the underlying problems that the measure is describing. This and other people-related issues must be resolved [Carey67, Grady87]. For example, if you measure the number of lines of code developed each day, the people being measured must understand exactly how the data will be used and maintain a consistent counting method. We once saw a programmer copy dummy code into a program and add jumps around it just to make the line-count numbers rise; this is clearly not what was hoped when instituting the measure.

Balanced metrics are a common solution to offset measurement side effects. For example, it is common for organizations that use frameworks to set targets such as *Adopt 50 percent of all CMM Level 2 practices by December*. Without a balancing metric, it may be tempting for a project team to implement the easiest 50 percent of the elements in the framework (such as writing policy statements and processes), and avoid the 50 percent that may be harder to define and implement but have the most impact on the success of the project. This adoption metric can be balanced with one that tracks progress toward a business goal (for example, *Reduce defects reported from the field by 30 percent* or *Ensure product deliveries are no more than 15 percent late*). Tracking and correlating multiple indicators show whether progress is being made on issues that impact the business.

When you establish measures, allow time for refinement so that they reflect the results you are trying to measure. For example, the organization that plotted the percentage of project time spent in rework (Figure 3–3) redefined the word "rework" several times as they worked through their defect list. Toward the end of the list, the company reevaluated some defects as enhancement requests and recounted them as "new development," whereas they counted others that impacted program operation as defects requiring rework. These refinements in counting rules required several revisions to the graph.

When choosing your measures, communicate their intended use, refine them, and be aware of the side effects you may be introducing.

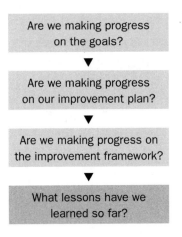

WHAT LESSONS HAVE WE LEARNED SO FAR?

If you want to learn how the improvement program is going, talk to the people who are being asked to change their behaviors and adopt new practices. This might include managers, developers, SQA personnel, and testers. Lessons learned feedback is not numeric, but it can provide ideas that prompt actions and complement the data from the other measures you have adopted.

Lessons learned data comes from interviewing individuals or using discussion groups. You can conduct a lessons learned session at any time; however, three specific times are particularly useful: when a goal has been reached, when an intermediate goal has been reached, and when the improvement effort hits an obstacle.

You can use the agenda in Figure 3–12 to determine lessons learned and related corrective actions. As a rule-of-thumb, break the session into segments of two hours or less to avoid team fatigue. When using group interviews, construct the groups to encourage uninhibited discussion. Invite people who are willing to be frank and candid. Select a good objective facilitator, someone not in charge of the improvement effort.

To stimulate the discussion, consider the following questions:

• Were the improvement activities tied to the business goals and problems experienced by the organization?

• Was there enough effort invested to adopt the new or improved techniques?

• Were new practices tailored appropriately to the needs of each project? Were pilot projects used to ensure their appropriateness?

Lessons learned agenda
1. Clarify the scope of the session.
2. Determine strengths (what went well).
3. Determine areas for improvement.
4. Set priorities.
5. Determine corrective actions.

Figure 3–12   Lessons learned agenda.

- Is there evidence that the results of the organization are improving? (This can include anecdotal stories as well as metrics.)

Here is an example of this process for a complete execution of the improvement cycle. We have explained the lessons in more detail here than would be typical during a brainstorming session involving people familiar with the issues. The data in this example comes from one division of a large multinational company that produces software for digital image processing equipment.

1. Clarify the scope of the session.

Capture the lessons learned from one complete execution of the improvement cycle

2. Determine strengths (what went well).

Lesson 1: Decentralizing the action plan gives each project team ownership over its plan.

- The centralized action plan for the division was split into three separate plans. When each plan addressed a single product line's specific goals and problems, the project teams became excited about the improvement program.

Lesson 2: Break the action plan into small chunks and just start.

- Starting with an overwhelming list of problems, we decided to focus on the immediate issues that were impacting projects A and B. This included auditing the release process, inspecting critical code, and consolidating our two defect tracking systems used by the developers and the help desk. Starting on a small scale gave our improvement program momentum, something it had never had before.

Lesson 3: Don't preach when an example can say everything for you.

- The improvement team had been pushing risk management for six months with little impact. When the project manager of our smallest project described at a division meeting how risk management techniques were used to turn his project around from near disaster, other project teams started using the process.

Lesson 4: Do not struggle for too long; get some help.

- We knew we wanted to work on project planning, but the teams would either not make the time for planning, or they would plan to the point of overkill. If they planned too much, they threw up their hands and said that planning was not practical. We brought in an outside coach to help us plan two important releases and get back on the right track. The teams now understand what level of planning is appropriate.

Lesson 5: Guide people in applying each new technique to their work. People have so much going on they do not know where to start.

- When we deployed the inspection technique, people resisted because they said they had too much code to inspect. We developed guidelines to help them select appropriate sections of code and documentation for inspection. Each team picked 20 percent of its new work that matched at least one of the following criteria:
  - The most critical to the program's operation
  - The most used section in the product

- The most costly if defects were to exist
- The most error-prone section
- The least well-known section
- The most frequently changed section

• Similarly, when we deployed the estimation technique, people resisted because they said they had too much work to estimate. We developed guidelines to help them select appropriate sections of their project for the estimation process. Each team selected project components that matched at least one of the following criteria:

- The component is high risk (either difficult technically, critical to the success of the project, or full of unknowns).
- There is no historical estimate data on which to base our estimates.
- There are many varying opinions about how much work the component will take and the development approach that should be used.

Lesson 6: Focus all new techniques on the needs of the project.

• The techniques we deployed initially did not stick. The project team members did not see how the techniques would help them with their current issues. To address this problem, we started every improvement deployment session with a quick review of the project's top three problems and top three goals. During the deployment session, we allowed the team members to question where and when the new technique would help them on their "top six list." The project members could always see how the new technique applied to their current work.

Lesson 7: Obtain management buy-in for the plan before execution.

◆ The improvement team developed an action plan with some participation from the developers. Nevertheless, execution of the plan during the implementation phase was hopeless. No one had time to implement the plan, and the management team treated the improvement effort as a task to avoid at all costs. After six months, the improvement team was ready to give up.

Finally, one improvement team member asked the management team members what they would like to see changed in the improvement program. The clear message was that they felt that the improvements were being forced on them. In hindsight, the improvement team was in a rush to have the processes adopted and did not take the time to allow the managers to critique the plan or the proposed solutions before deployment.

Lesson 8: Keep measuring defect density and end user customer satisfaction.

◆ We measured product defect density (the number of defects found by the users for each release) and end user customer satisfaction. These numbers are now shared with our customers. Communicating this information has built an excellent trust level with our customer base. We have enduring metrics that guide our improvement program.

3. Determine areas for improvement.[7]

Lesson 9: The process-centric approach was very difficult to sell.

---

7. Corrective actions for these lessons are shown later in this chapter.

- The plans were initially organized around the key process areas of the CMM, and the process improvement team spent most of its time generating excessive documentation. The engineers and managers avoided the improvement effort at all costs.

Lesson 10: Using the same communication technique as everyone else allows the message to be lost.

- Each developer was receiving 200 to 300 e-mail messages each week related to his regular project work. Getting our improvement message out using e-mail to the project teams was impossible.

Lesson 11: Allowing private data to become public sets perilous expectations.

- We started to measure how many projects satisfied the CMM Level 2 activities using the mini-assessment process. One time we released project-specific data to some senior managers because we were trying to be helpful to the management team. That set the precedent for future mini-assessments. Projects became focused on the "score." We are now truly in a score-focused mess.

Lesson 12: Be careful of what information you ask for!

- We wanted to encourage people to put their sample process documents into the process assets library (PAL), so we measured the percentage of projects that submitted documents to the PAL. This measurement caused projects to submit everything they had to the PAL to earn extra credit. Now the measurement is meaningless and the PAL is completely full with who knows what.

Lesson 13: Using a scoring system for process adoption can encourage inappropriate behavior.

- We measured how many inspections (peer reviews) each team performed annually. To maintain our ISO9001 registration, we established a minimum requirement for each team to conduct two inspections annually. Now many teams refuse to do more than two each year. The benefit of finding defects has been replaced by the requirement to perform the minimum number of inspections.

4. Set priorities.

You can determine lessons learned priorities using a process similar to the one described in Chapter 1 for setting goal priorities (Table 1–3). Table 3–2 uses a scale of 1 through 10 (1 = low benefit, 10 = high benefit) to estimate the relative benefits of maintaining each strength and implementing each area for improvement. Rating each item relative to the other items on the list allows you to order the list in the absence of hard benefit data. If you have data, such as the time or money saved by adopting the lesson, then substitute this data for the relative benefit number. Similarly, Table 3–2 uses a scale to estimate the relative costs of maintaining each strength and implementing each area for improvement. If it exists, substitute hard data for the relative cost rating.

The last step in prioritization is to order the lessons by the improvement phase in which they would be adopted. Table 3–2 shows an example of this prioritization scheme with the last column stating the phase where the lesson would be considered.

5. Determine corrective actions.

If you have many lessons learned, consider developing detailed corrective actions only for the lessons that have the highest priority. Corrective actions include tasks to maintain a strength that is already in place and tasks to prevent the occurrence of a negative lesson. For example, lesson 5 in Table 3–2 says, *Guide people in applying each new technique to their work*. Tasks to

Table 3–2 Prioritization Scheme for Lessons Learned

No.	Lessons Learned (Strength [S] or Area for Improvement [I])	Relative Benefit of Maintaining/ Implementing Lesson Learned, 1–10 pts	Relative Cost of Maintaining/ Implementing Lesson Learned, 1–10 pts	Priority (Benefit/ Cost)	Corrective Actions	The Improvement Phase Where These Corrective Actions Should Be Used
1	Decentralizing the action plan gives each project team ownership over its plan [S].	8	4	2	Continue having three separate action plans, one for each of the three product lines.	Planning
2	Break the action plan into small chunks and just start [S].	8	2	4	Focus the improvement-planning phase on the organization's problems and goals. Pick the top two problems and start.	Planning
3	Don't preach when an example can say everything for you [S].	8	2	4	Have one project each month conduct a one-hour briefing describing the use and benefits of a new technique.	Implementing

continued

Table 3-2 Prioritization Scheme for Lessons Learned *continued*

No.	Lessons Learned (Strength [S] or Area for Improvement [I])	Relative Benefit of Maintaining/ Implementing Lesson Learned, 1–10 pts	Relative Cost of Maintaining/ Implementing Lesson Learned, 1–10 pts	Priority (Benefit/ Cost)	Corrective Actions	The Improvement Phase Where These Corrective Actions Should Be Used
4	Do not struggle for too long; get some help [S].	6	–	–	No action at this time. Keep this lesson in mind for when we hit trouble again.	Implementing
5	Guide people in applying each new technique to their work. People have so much going on they do not know where to start [S].	9	6	1.5	For each process in the process assets library (PAL), add tailoring guidelines to explain when the process should be used. Provide one-on-one coaching to new project teams.	Implementing
6	Focus all new techniques on the needs of the project [S].	10	1	10	Continue to do a quick review of each project's top three problems and goals before each improvement coaching session starts.	Implementing

#						
7	Obtain management buy-in for the plan before execution [S].	8	2	4	Have the management team review the next action plan to obtain buy-in and understanding. Invite managers to participate in the next planning cycle.	Planning
8	Keep measuring defect density and end user customer satisfaction [S].	8	1	8	Do not change anything.	Checking
9	The process-centric approach was very difficult to sell [I].	9	1	9	Focus the improvement-planning phase on the organization's problems and goals.	Planning
10	Using the same communication technique as everyone else allows the message to be lost [I].	7	3	2.3	Use bright pink 8.5 × 11-inch newsletters, one-on-one sessions, and pizza lunches to communicate our services and stories.	Implementing

continued

111

Table 3–2 Prioritization Scheme for Lessons Learned *continued*

No.	Lessons Learned (Strength [S] or Area for Improvement [I])	Relative Benefit of Maintaining/ Implementing Lesson Learned, 1–10 pts	Relative Cost of Maintaining/ Implementing Lesson Learned, 1–10 pts	Priority (Benefit/ Cost)	Corrective Actions	The Improvement Phase Where These Corrective Actions Should Be Used
11	Allowing private data to become public sets perilous expectations [I].	8	3	2.6	Brief management on the current metrics program and tell them what data we plan to communicate. Explain that making private data public often results in data degradation because people can focus on optimizing the score and not address the underlying problems.	Planning
12	Be careful of what information you ask for [I].	9	6	1.5	Look at the current PAL and delete unused material. Don't measure the percentage of projects that submitted documents to the PAL.	Planning
13	Using a scoring system for process adoption can encourage inappropriate behavior [I].	7	5	1.4	Look at all the metrics again and determine which ones can be optimized but lead to little benefit for the organization. Fix poor metrics. Educate the organization on the intent and correct use of metrics.	Checking

maintain this strength include making guidelines available to new users of each process, and providing one-on-one coaching to help project team members learn a new technique quickly with less frustration.

SUMMARY

Checking progress is an essential activity that provides the organization with feedback during execution of an improvement program. Metrics derived from the business goals form a primary source of information for verifying progress and guiding improvement activities. If you are using an improvement framework (for example, CMMI), you can use mini-assessments to measure adoption of the practices within the framework. Lessons learned data from the people who are improving provides additional feedback to monitor the effectiveness of the improvement program.

Each metric provides a view of progress and indicates when corrective actions are needed. Examples of corrective actions include revising one section of the action plan to help achieve a goal that has not currently been met, or communicating the status of a stalled improvement program to senior management with the aim of reigniting it.

Quick Start

◆ If you have not already done so, obtain a baseline for a few key metrics so you can gauge progress from where you started.

◆ Pick one goal and construct a simple trend line that shows the goal and where you are now relative to that goal.

◆ Select one goal in your original action plan that is not yet complete. Determine if corrective actions are needed to move you closer to that goal.

◆ If your improvement program is already well underway, conduct a mini-assessment for a project to assess its current progress and next steps. Expand the mini-assessment to all projects every four to six months.

◆ Discuss lessons learned regarding your improvement program with some of the program's participants.

Conclusion

Changing the results of an organization can be a daunting task. The greatest challenge is knowing what to work on and where to start. By following a few simple steps, you can plan and manage an effective improvement program. The essence of everything we have said is to start small and make all improvements useful. Your job is to create and sustain this environment.

We hope this book has given you some key steps for your improvement program. Don't be surprised if you need to pick up and reread the book after you have worked though your first improvement cycle. All new skills take practice.

If you would like to share your stories, please contact us at help@processgroup.com.

APPENDIX A

Mapping Goals and Problems to CMM (v1.1)

MAPPING EXAMPLE USING THE GOALS AND PROBLEMS LISTED IN CHAPTER 1 (TABLE 1–2)

Goal	CMM (v1.1) Key Process Area Elements That Would Help[1]
1. Meet all our cost and schedule commitments.	
Problem 7: Finding time to do critical activities (product development) is difficult. Time is spent on crisis activities.	Level 2: Software Project Planning (SPP) activities 4, 10, and 12
Problem 11: Revising the project plan is difficult. Items drop off, new things are added, plan is out of date.	Level 2: SPP activity 6; Software Project Tracking and Oversight (SPTO) activities 2, 8, and 9
Problem 12: We don't understand our capacity and do not have one list of all the work we have to do.	Level 2: SPP activity 7; abilities 1 and 4

1. The mapping is focused primarily on CMM Level 2 management practices to address fundamental planning and configuration management problems. This organization was not ready for more advanced Level 3 engineering practices. Adoption of the Level 3 elements listed in the table was delayed until project management and configuration management were in place. The CMM activities and practices are defined in the second part of Appendix A.

117

Goal	CMM (v1.1) Key Process Area Elements That Would Help
Problem 13: Schedule tracking and communication of changes to affected groups is poor.	Level 2: SPTO activities 3, 4, 6, 8, 9, 12, and 13
Problem 14: Testers do not have tools to manage their test activities.	Level 2: SPP activity 14 Level 3: Software Product Engineering (SPE) activity 1
2. Deliver product X by mm/dd/yy.	
Problem 1: Need better requirements. Requirements tracking not in place. Changes to requirements are not tracked; code does not match specification at test time.	Level 2: Requirements Management (RM) activities 1, 2, and 3; ability 2
Problem 2: Management direction unclear for product version 2.3. Goals change often.	Level 2: RM activities 1 and 3; verification 1
3. Reduce rework to less than 20 percent of total project effort.	
Problem 3: Quality department does not have training in product and test skills.	Level 2: Software Quality Assurance (SQA) abilities 2 and 3
Problem 4: Unclear status of software changes.	Level 2: Software Configuration Management (SCM) activities 8 and 9, ability 1
Problem 5: Lack of resources and skills allocated to software design.	Level 2: SPP activity 10 Level 3: SPE activity 3; abilities 1 and 2
Problem 6: Changes to specifications and documentation are not communicated effectively to documentation and test groups.	Level 2: RM activities 1, 2, and 3; SCM activities 5, 6, and 9, and ability 1

Goal		CMM (v1.1) Key Process Area Elements That Would Help
Problem 8:	Test plan does not necessarily encompass things that matter to the customer.	Level 3: SPE activities 5, 6, and 7
Problem 9:	Defect repairs break essential product features.	Level 2: SCM activities 5, 6, 7, 9, and 10; abilities 1, 2, 4, and 5; verification 3 and 4
Problem 10:	Wrong files (for example, dynamic link libraries) are put on CD. Unsure of the correct ones.	Level 2: SCM activities 4, 7, 8, 9, and 10, and verification 3

4. **Improve the performance of our core software product. (Target to be defined.)**

Level 2: SPP activity 11; SPTO activity 7

5. **Achieve customer rating of 9/10 on product evaluation form.**

Problem 15:	Customers are unhappy. There are approximately 300 outstanding defects that have not been addressed.	Level 2: RM activities 1, 2, and 3, and abilities 1 and 2; SCM activity 5

6. **Keep profits at 15 percent (and costs at the same level as last year).**

Level 2: SPP activities 10, 12, and 13; SPTO activities 6, 10, and 11; SQA activity 2

DEFINITIONS OF CMM1.1 LEVEL 2 AND LEVEL 3 ACTIVITIES USED IN MAPPING

Requirements Management (RM)—Level 2

Activity 1	The software engineering group reviews the allocated requirements before they are incorporated into the software project.

Activity 2	The software engineering group uses the allocated requirements as the basis for software plans, work products, and activities.
Activity 3	Changes to the allocated requirements are reviewed and incorporated into the software project.
Ability 1	For each project, responsibility is established for analyzing the system requirements and allocating them to hardware, software, and other system components.
Ability 2	The allocated requirements are documented.
Verification 1	The activities for managing the allocated requirements are reviewed with senior management on a periodic basis.

Software Configuration Management (SCM)—Level 2

Activity 4	The software work products to be placed under configuration management are identified.
Activity 5	Change requests and problem reports for all configuration items/units are initiated, recorded, reviewed, approved, and tracked according to a documented procedure.
Activity 6	Changes to baselines are controlled according to a documented procedure.
Activity 7	Products from the software baseline library are created and their release is controlled according to a documented procedure.
Activity 8	The status of configuration items/units is recorded according to a documented procedure.
Activity 9	Standard reports documenting the SCM activities and the contents of the software baseline are developed and made available to affected groups and individuals.
Activity 10	Software baseline audits are conducted according to a documented procedure.
Ability 1	A board having the authority for managing the project's software baselines (in other words, a software configuration control board—SCCB) exists or is established.
Ability 2	A group that is responsible for coordinating and implementing SCM for the project (in other words, the SCM group) exists.

Ability 4	Members of the SCM group are trained in the objectives, procedures, and methods for performing their SCM activities.
Ability 5	Members of the software engineering group and other software-related groups are trained to perform their SCM activities.
Verification 3	The SCM group periodically audits software baselines to verify that they conform to the documentation that defines them.
Verification 4	The Software Quality Assurance group reviews and/or audits the activities and work products for SCM and reports the results.
Software Project Planning (SPP)—Level 2	
Activity 4	Software project commitments made to individuals and groups external to the organization are reviewed with senior management according to a documented procedure.
Activity 6	The project's software development plan is developed according to a documented procedure.
Activity 7	The plan for the software project is documented.
Activity 10	Estimates for the software project's effort and costs are derived according to a documented procedure.
Activity 11	Estimates for the project's critical computer resources are derived according to a documented procedure.
Activity 12	The project's software schedule is derived according to a documented procedure.
Activity 13	The software risks associated with the cost, resource, schedule, and technical aspects of the project are identified, assessed, and documented.
Activity 14	Plans for the project's software engineering facilities and support tools are prepared.
Ability 1	A documented and approved statement of work exists for the software project.
Ability 4	The software managers, software engineers, and other individuals involved in the software project planning are trained in the software estimating and planning procedures applicable to their areas of responsibility.

Software Project Tracking and Oversight (SPTO)—Level 2	
Activity 2	The project's software development plan is revised according to a documented procedure.
Activity 3	Software project commitments and changes to commitments made to individuals and groups external to the organization are reviewed with senior management according to a documented procedure.
Activity 4	Approved changes to commitments that affect the software project are communicated to the members of the software engineering group and other software-related groups.
Activity 6	The project's software effort and costs are tracked, and corrective actions are taken as necessary.
Activity 7	The project's critical computer resources are tracked, and corrective actions are taken as necessary.
Activity 8	The project's software schedule is tracked, and corrective actions are taken as necessary.
Activity 9	Software engineering technical activities are tracked, and corrective actions are taken as necessary.
Activity 10	The software risks associated with the cost, resource, schedule, and technical aspects of the project are tracked.
Activity 11	Actual measurement data and replanning data for the software project are recorded.
Activity 12	The software engineering group conducts periodic internal reviews to track technical progress, plans, performance, and issues against the software development plan.
Activity 13	Formal reviews to address the accomplishments and results of the software project are conducted at selected project milestones according to a documented procedure.
Software Quality Assurance (SQA)—Level 2	
Activity 2	The SQA group's activities are performed in accordance with the SQA plan.
Ability 2	Adequate resources and funding are provided for performing the SQA activities.
Ability 3	Members of the SQA group are trained to perform their SQA activities.

Software Product Engineering (SPE)—Level 3	
Activity 1	Appropriate software engineering methods and tools are integrated into the project's defined software process.
Activity 3	The software design is developed, maintained, documented, and verified according to the project's defined software process to accommodate the software requirements and to form the framework for coding.
Activity 5	Software testing is performed according to the project's defined software process.
Activity 6	Integration testing of the software is planned and performed according to the project's defined software process.
Activity 7	System and acceptance testing of the software are planned and performed to demonstrate that the software satisfies its requirements.
Ability 1	Adequate resources and funding are provided for performing the software engineering tasks.
Ability 2	Members of the software engineering technical staff receive required training to perform their technical assignments.

APPENDIX B

Mapping Goals and Problems to CMM (v1.1) and CMMI Systems Engineering/Software Engineering/Integrated Product and Process Development, version 1.1 (SE/SW/IPPD, v1.1)

MAPPING EXAMPLE USING THE GOALS AND PROBLEMS LISTED IN CHAPTER 1 (FIGURES 1–5)

Goal: Reduce release cycle to six to nine months for product *X*.		
Problem	**SEI CMM (v1.1) Key Process Area Elements That Would Help[1]**	**SEI CMMI-SE/SW/ IPPD (v1.1) Process Area Elements That Would Help[1]**
1. Changing requirements	Level 2: Requirements Management (RM) activities 1, 2, and 3; Software Configuration Management (SCM) activity 5; ability 1	Level 2: RM specific practices 1.3, 1.4, and 1.5; Configuration Management (CM) specific practices 1.2, 1.3, 2.1, and 2.2

---

1. These mappings include Level 2 management and Level 3 engineering practices from CMM (v1.1) and CMMI-SE/SW/IPPD (v1.1), respectively. This organization had good project management in place and was ready for more advanced engineering practices. The activities and practices are defined in the second half of Appendix B.

Problem	SEI CMM (v1.1) Key Process Area Elements That Would Help	SEI CMMI-SE/SW/IPPD (v1.02) Process Area Elements That Would Help
2. Loss of resources; difficult to replace people with specialized skills who leave the project	Level 2: Software Project and Tracking Oversight (SPTO) activities 2 and 8 Level 3: Training Program (TP) activity 1; Software Product Engineering (SPE) abilities 1 and 2	Level 2: Project Monitoring and Control (PMC) specific practices 1.6 and 2.1 Level 3: Organizational Training (OT) specific practices 1.1, 1.2, and 2.1; Technical Solution (TS) generic practice 2.5
3. Too many features for the six- to nine-month development cycle	Level 2: Software Project Planning (SPP) activities 4, 12, and 13 Level 3: SPE activity 2	Level 2: Project Planning (PP) specific practices 1.1, 2.1, 2.2, 3.2, and 3.3 Level 3: Requirements Development (RD) specific practices 3.3 and 3.4
4. Poor quality of incoming code from other groups	Level 3: Intergroup Coordination (IC) activities 2, 5, and 6; Peer Review (PR) activities 1 and 2, ability 1	Level 3: Integrated Project Management (IPM) specific practices 2.2 and 2.3; Verification (VER) specific practice 2.2; Product Integration (PI) specific practice 3.1
5. Inadequate availability of test equipment	Level 2: SPP activities 13 and 14 Level 3: SPE activities 6 and 7	Level 2: PP specific practices 2.2 and 2.4 Level 3: Validation (VAL) specific practice 1.2
6. Lack of visibility within each life cycle phase; it is difficult to know whether we are ahead or behind schedule	Level 3: Integrated Software Management (ISM) activities 4, 7, and 11, and verification 2	Level 3: IPM specific practices 1.1 and 1.4

Problem	SEI CMM (v1.1) Key Process Area Elements That Would Help	SEI CMMI-SE/SW/IPPD (v1.1) Process Area Elements That Would Help
7. Don't always have the resources available to complete the planned work	Level 2: SPP activities 4 and 13; SPTO activity 8 Level 3: ISM activities 3, 5, 10, and 11	Level 2: PP specific practices 1.1, 2.1, 2.2, 3.2, and 3.3 Level 3: IPM specific practices 1.2 and 1.4; Risk Management (RMAN) specific practice 3.1
8. Difficult to find defects early	Level 3: PR activities 1 and 2, and ability 1.	Level 3: VER specific practices 2.2 and 3.1; generic practice 2.3

DEFINITIONS OF CMM1.1 LEVEL 2 AND LEVEL 3 ACTIVITIES USED IN MAPPING

Requirements Management (RM)—Level 2

Activity 1	The software engineering group reviews the allocated requirements before they are incorporated into the software project.
Activity 2	The software engineering group uses the allocated requirements as the basis for software plans, work products, and activities.
Activity 3	Changes to the allocated requirements are reviewed and incorporated into the software project.

Software Configuration Management (SCM)—Level 2

Activity 5	Change requests and problem reports for all configuration items/units are initiated, recorded, reviewed, approved, and tracked according to a documented procedure.
Ability 1	A board having the authority for managing the project's software baselines (in other words, a software configuration control board—SCCB) exists or is established.

Software Project Planning (SPP)—Level 2	
Activity 4	Software project commitments made to individuals and groups external to the organization are reviewed with senior management according to a documented procedure.
Activity 12	The project's software schedule is derived according to a documented procedure.
Activity 13	The software risks associated with the cost, resource, schedule, and technical aspects of the project are identified, assessed, and documented.
Activity 14	Plans for the project's software engineering facilities and support tools are prepared.
Software Project Tracking and Oversight (SPTO)—Level 2	
Activity 2	The project's software development plan is revised according to a documented procedure.
Activity 8	The project's software schedule is tracked, and corrective actions are taken as necessary.
Training Program (TP)—Level 3	
Activity 1	Each software project develops and maintains a training plan that specifies its training needs.
Software Product Engineering (SPE)—Level 3	
Ability 1	Adequate resources and funding are provided for performing the software engineering tasks.
Ability 2	Members of the software engineering technical staff receive required training to perform their technical assignments.
Activity 2	The software requirements are developed, maintained, documented, and verified by systematically analyzing the allocated requirements according to the defined software process.
Activity 6	Integration testing of the software is planned and performed according to the project's defined software process.
Activity 7	System and acceptance testing of the software are planned and performed to demonstrate that the software satisfies its requirements.

Intergroup Coordination (IC)—Level 3	
Activity 2	Representatives of the project's software engineering group work with representatives of the other engineering groups to monitor and coordinate technical activities and to resolve technical issues.
Activity 5	Work products produced as input to other engineering groups are reviewed by representatives of the receiving groups to ensure that the work products meet their needs.
Activity 6	Intergroup issues not resolved by the individual representatives of the project engineering groups are handled according to a documented procedure.
Peer Reviews (PR)—Level 3	
Activity 1	Peer reviews are planned and the plans are documented.
Activity 2	Peer reviews are performed according to a documented procedure.
Ability 1	Adequate resources and funding are provided for performing peer reviews on each software work product to be reviewed.
Integrated Software Management (ISM)—Level 3	
Activity 3	The project's software development plan, which describes the use of the project's defined software process, is developed and revised according to a documented procedure.
Activity 4	The software project is managed in accordance with the project's defined software process.
Activity 5	The organization's software process database is used for software planning and estimating.
Activity 7	The project's software effort and costs are managed according to a documented procedure.
Activity 10	The project's software risks are identified, assessed, documented, and managed according to a documented procedure.
Activity 11	Reviews of the software project are periodically performed to determine the actions needed to bring the software project's performance and results in line with the current and projected needs of the business, customer, and end users, as appropriate.

| Verification 2 | The activities for managing the software project are reviewed with the project manager on both a periodic and event-driven basis. |

DEFINITIONS OF CMMI-SE/SW/IPPD (STAGED V1.02) LEVEL 2 AND LEVEL 3 ACTIVITIES USED IN MAPPING

Requirements Management (RM)—Level 2	
Specific practice 1.3	Manage changes to the requirements as they evolve during the project.
Specific practice 1.4	Maintain bidirectional traceability among the requirements and the project plans and work products.
Specific practice 1.5	Identify inconsistencies between the project plans and work products and the requirements.

Configuration Management (CM)—Level 2	
Specific practice 1.2	Establish and maintain a configuration management and change management system for controlling work products.
Specific practice 1.3	Create or release baselines for internal use and for delivery to the customer.
Specific practice 2.1	Track change requests for the configuration items.
Specific practice 2.2	Control changes to the content of configuration items.

Project Planning (PP)—Level 2	
Specific practice 1.1	Establish and maintain a top-level work breakdown structure (WBS) to estimate of the scope of the project.
Specific practice 2.1	Establish and maintain the project's budget and schedule.
Specific practice 2.2	Identify and analyze project risks.
Specific practice 2.4	Plan for necessary resources to perform the project.

Specific practice 3.2	Reconcile the project plan to reflect available and projected resources.
Specific practice 3.3	Obtain commitment from relevant stakeholders responsible for performing and supporting plan execution.

Project Monitoring and Control (PMC)—Level 2

Specific practice 1.6	Periodically review the project's progress, performance, and issues.
Specific practice 2.1	Collect and analyze the issues and determine the corrective actions necessary to address the issues.

Organizational Training (OT)—Level 3

Specific practice 1.1	Establish and maintain the strategic training needs of the organization.
Specific practice 1.2	Determine which training needs are the responsibility of the organization and which will be left to the individual project or support group.
Specific practice 2.1	Deliver the training following the organizational training tactical plan.

Technical Solution (TS)—Level 3

Generic practice 2.5	Train the people performing or supporting the technical solution process as needed.

Requirements Development (RD)—Level 3

Specific practice 3.3	Analyze requirements to ensure that they are necessary and sufficient.
Specific practice 3.4	Analyze requirements to balance stakeholder needs and constraints.

Verification (VER)—Level 3

Specific practice 2.2	Conduct peer reviews on selected work products and identify issues resulting from the peer review.
Specific practice 3.1	Perform verification on selected work products.
Generic practice 2.3	Provide adequate resources for performing the verification process, developing the work products, and providing the services of the process.

Validation (VAL)—Level 3	
Specific practice 1.2	Establish and maintain the environment needed to support validation.
Integrated Project Management (IPM)—Level 3	
Specific practice 1.1	Establish and maintain the project's defined process.
Specific practice 1.2	Use the organizational process assets and measurement repository for estimating and planning the project's activities.
Specific practice 1.4	Manage the project using the project plan, the other plans that affect the project, and the project's defined process.
Specific practice 2.2	Participate with relevant stakeholders to identify, negotiate, and track critical dependencies.
Specific practice 2.3	Resolve issues with relevant stakeholders.
Risk Management (RMAN)—Level 3	
Specific practice 3.1	Develop a risk mitigation plan for the most important risks to the project, as defined by the risk management strategy.
Product Integration (PI)—Level 3	
Specific practice 3.1	Confirm, prior to assembly, that each product component required to assemble the product has been properly identified, functions according to its description, and that the product-component interfaces comply with the interface descriptions.

APPENDIX C

Action Plan Example

Action Plan Owner: ___Jane___

Primary Goal and Intermediate Goals (The results you want)	Purpose of Goal (Why do you want to achieve the goal?)	Actions	Priority (*essential)
Reduce product development cycle to six to nine months for product X	**Deliver earlier than competition**		
Manage changing requirements (based on problem 1).	Prevent schedule slips resulting from expensive scope changes.	Only allow changes to the application interface, not to the kernel routines.	1*
		Establish a group with the authority for managing the project's software baselines.	2*
		Check progress and take corrective action.	—
		Improve the library control system to minimize version control errors. Investigate requirements management tools.	3

133

Primary Goal and Intermediate Goals (The results you want)	Purpose of Goal (Why do you want to achieve the goal?)	Actions	Priority (*essential)
		Record and track change requests and problem reports for all configuration items.	4
		Review the initial requirements and changes before they are incorporated into the project plan.	5
		Baseline the requirements before design commences.	6
Replace people with specialized skills who leave the project (based on problem 2).	Attrition causes people with critical skills to leave the project, causing multiple lengthy relearning cycles.	Train the technical staff to perform their assignments.	1*
		Revise the project's software development plan and escalate staffing issues that need corrective actions.	2*
		Check progress and take corrective action.	—
		Maintain a training plan that specifies training needs for each project member.	3
Set feature priorities for a six- to nine-month development cycle (based on problem 3).	Ensure commitments are achievable.	Establish a review process with clients to negotiate features for a six- to nine-month development cycle.	1*

Primary Goal and Intermediate Goals (The results you want)	Purpose of Goal (Why do you want to achieve the goal?)	Actions	Priority (*essential)
		Rate each feature based on value to the customer (1–10 points) and cost to develop (1–10 points).	2*
		Check progress and take corrective action.	—
		Review project commitments with senior managers, engineers, and the customer to obtain agreement.	3
		Perform risk management related to the schedule, resource, and technical aspects of the project.	4
		Establish an incremental delivery plan to phase in lower priority features.	5
Improve quality of incoming code from other groups (based on problem 4).	Reduce major delays when defects are found very late in code used from other projects.	Improve unit testing for incoming code; make it more efficient.	1*
		Review incoming work products produced by other groups to ensure that they meet our needs. Conduct inspections (peer reviews) following the Gilb inspection process [Gilb93].	2*
		Check progress and take corrective action.	—

Primary Goal and Intermediate Goals (The results you want)	Purpose of Goal (Why do you want to achieve the goal?)	Actions	Priority (*essential)
		Perform integration testing of incoming code.	3
Ensure adequate availability of test equipment (based on problem 5).	Avoid delays in schedule caused by waiting for test equipment availability.	Develop a plan for the project's software test equipment tools (unit testing, system testing, integration testing).	1*
		Check progress and take corrective action.	—
		Identify the software risks associated with acquiring test equipment. Communicate the impact of not having the necessary equipment.	2
Improve visibility within all life cycle phases (based on problem 6).	Detect problems early that snowball.	Conduct project phase reviews to determine the actions needed to bring the software project's performance in line with the current/projected needs of the business, customer, and end users.	1*
		Follow a software life cycle with predefined stages of manageable size.	2*
		Check progress and take corrective action.	—
		Adopt earned value tracking.	3
		Review the activities for managing the software project with management.	4

Primary Goal and Intermediate Goals (The results you want)	Purpose of Goal (Why do you want to achieve the goal?)	Actions	Priority (*essential)
Ensure resources are available to complete the planned work (based on problem 7).	Prevent delays caused by roaming resources.	Develop a complete software development plan.	1*
		Review project commitments made to individuals and groups external to the project with senior management.	2*
		Identify risks associated with the cost, resource, schedule, and technical aspects of the project. Report risks and mitigation actions to management.	3*
		Check progress and take corrective action.	—
		Use the company scheduling process to derive the project's software schedule.	4
		Perform reviews of the software project periodically to determine the actions needed to bring the software project's performance and results in line with the current/projected needs of the business, customer, and end users.	5

Primary Goal and Intermediate Goals (The results you want)	Purpose of Goal (Why do you want to achieve the goal?)	Actions	Priority (*essential)
Find defects earlier (based on problem 8).	Detect bad requirements that enter development. Detect design flaws that enter the coding phase. Detect coding defects that cause the test phase to come to a halt.	Negotiate time for inspections in the schedule.	1*
		Add inspections to the project plan.	2*
		Conduct inspections using the Gilb inspection process on all major work products [Gilb93]. Focus initially on critical documents and code.	3*
		Check progress and take corrective action.	—

APPENDIX D
Risk Management Plan Example

Risk Items (potential future problems derived from the brainstorming session)	Consequence if Risk Item Does Occur	Likelihood of Risk Item Occurring	Impact to Project if Risk Item Does Occur	Priority (Likelihood × Impact)	Actions to Reduce Likelihood of Risk Occurring	Actions to Reduce Impact if Risk Does Occur
Management buy-in for improvement diminishes.	Improvement program fails.	9	10	90	Ensure that the improvement program addresses the management team's problems and goals. Establish a steering committee to oversee the improvement effort. Meet bimonthly. Publicize early results to management. Provide four funding options for the improvement program: full-time, part-time, short bursts, and investment spread over two years.	Determine improvements that can be made at a project level without major funding. Explain the problems and goals that will not be addressed because of reduced funding. Determine a time when the improvement program can be revisited.

Risk	Consequence				Action Plan	
Management changes priorities before we complete any milestone.	Improvement program loses credibility.	9	9	81	Present the action plan to management and obtain agreement that priorities remain unchanged between major improvement milestones. Explain the problems and goals that will not be addressed if changes in priority occur.	Determine improvements that can be made regardless of which project is active.
New requirements management tool has long learning curve.	Developers give up in frustration.	9	8	72	Start a pilot project to test the tool. Select a subset of the tool's features to use. Have vendor come on-site to help transition to the tool.	Establish a cutoff date when we will give up on the tool and use manual methods instead. The tool can be used on the next release.
Library control person might leave.	Wasted time training a new person.	7	8	56	Extend contract of library control person. Determine incentives that could cause the person to stay.	Identify a local library control company that can temporarily take over library management if the library control person leaves. Bring the company up to speed now about current library structure.

Risk Items (potential future problems derived from the brainstorming session)	Consequence if Risk Item Does Occur	Likelihood of Risk Item Occurring	Impact to Project if Risk Item Does Occur	Priority (Likelihood × Impact)	Actions to Reduce Likelihood of Risk Occurring	Actions to Reduce Impact if Risk Does Occur
						Create a library design document that describes the library structure and important maintenance activities. Have the current library control person give a presentation on the current library structure to allow others to perform the task.
New group to manage baseline changes is not accepted by project managers.	Duplication of effort or baseline changes are not managed.	6	9	54	Form a focus group of project managers that need a baseline change group. Share current plans and revise plans to reduce risk of rejection. Seek other groups that have used similar techniques. Understand their lessons learned.	Identify a second, less formal approach (for example, change control process in word processor). Escalate rejection to management and explain that cycletime reduction will not improve until requirements changes are managed.

Creation of specialized training materials for new staff takes too long.	Improvement implementation delayed.	5	7	35	Split the training materials into three categories: essential, should be done, and wish list. Complete the essential materials first. Have them ready to ship by the deadline.
					Use slide presentation program for all specialized documentation so that it can be presented as a training class. Set a limit of 30 to 40 slides so that the training materials are concise. Limit the information included in the training materials. Convey the majority of the information verbally or through exercises.
Requirements management tool is delivered to us late.	Pass up the opportunity to try the tool.	4	3	12	Check with the supplier on shipment each week.
					Prepare for manual requirements management using a word processor, last year's version of the tool, or a competing tool.

APPENDIX E
Summary of SEI CMM (v1.1) and CMMI-SE/SW/IPPD (v1.1)

In 1993, the Software Engineering Institute (SEI) released version 1.1 of the Capability Maturity Model (CMM). The topics (key process areas) covered in the model are listed in Table E–1. A full description of the model is available at www.sei.cmu.edu and in [Paulk93]. Selected implementation examples are described in [Caputo98].

In 2000, the SEI released a revised version called CMM Integration (CMMI). CMMI combines three source models into a single model for use by organizations pursuing enterprisewide process improvement:

1. Capability Maturity Model for Software (SW-CMM v2.0, draft C)

2. Electronic Industries Alliance/Interim Standard (EIA/IS) 731

3. Integrated Product Development Capability Maturity Model (IPD-CMM, v0.98)

Table E–2 presents a summary. A full description of the model is available at www.sei.cmu.edu and [CMMI02].

Table E–1   Summary of SEI CMM (v1.1)

CMM (v1.1) Maturity Level	Key Process Area
1	No criteria
2	Software Configuration Management Software Quality Assurance Software Subcontract Management Software Project Tracking and Oversight Software Project Planning Requirements Management
3	Peer Reviews Intergroup Coordination Software Product Engineering Integrated Software Management Training Program Organization Process Definition Organization Process Focus
4	Software Quality Management Quantitative Process Management
5	Process Change Management Technology Change Management Defect Prevention

Table E–2 Summary of SEI CMMI-SE/SW/IPPD (v1.1)

CMMI-SE/SW/IPPD (v1.1) Maturity Level	Process Area
1	No criteria
2	Requirements Management Project Planning Project Monitoring and Control Supplier Agreement Management Measurement and Analysis Process and Product Quality Assurance Configuration Management
3	Requirements Development Technical Solution Product Integration Verification Validation Organizational Process Focus Organizational Process Definition Organizational Training Integrated Project Management for IPPD Risk Management Integrated Teaming Decision Analysis and Resolution Organizational Environment for Integration
4	Organizational Process Performance Quantitative Project Management
5	Organizational Innovation and Deployment Causal Analysis and Resolution

APPENDIX F
Mini-Assessment Process

One method of tracking progress of an organization against an improvement framework is a mini-assessment [Sakry93, Carr00]. A mini-assessment obtains a quick snapshot of your improvement program. A mini-assessment is not an audit [Jalote00, Humphrey89] or a full process assessment, but rather is a small check to determine progress. Results from the mini-assessment indicate how fast improvement is taking place so you can detect any backsliding.

A mini-assessment is a process-focused, not a goal-focused, progress check. Therefore, other goal-oriented metrics should accompany it so the mini-assessment is not the sole means of determining progress. When a process check is the sole measure of progress, it is easy for an organization to lose sight of the overall purpose of the improvement program and become overly focused on the process score. By adding business-oriented metrics such as product end user satisfaction and schedule predictability, an organization can balance metrics that track framework adoption with metrics that reflect business success.

Before conducting a mini-assessment, decide which practices you will check for adoption. These could include activities described by the organization's development life cycle, CMM, ISO9001, or another improvement framework. Develop a list of questions based on these criteria, typically one question for each practice. You can also include additional questions to verify that problems identified during previous assessments have been addressed. In the example in Figure F-1, the last question checks to

---

Sample mini-assessment questions

Describe how your team

- Performs inspections or walkthroughs for key work products (such as code, design, test cases, and test plans)
- Performs black-box testing
- Performs white-box testing
- Performs version control of all significant work products (from plans to code)

Do you have adequate computer network stability (compared with the problem reported in the last assessment)?

Figure F–1   Example of criteria for the mini-assessment.

see whether a previously identified network problem has been fixed.

There are seven steps to the mini-assessment process.

1. Plan the assessment.

2. Meet with the interviewees to explain what will be checked and how.

3. Perform the mini-assessment interview.

4. Communicate the results.

5. Debrief on the mini-assessment process.

6. Improve the questionnaire.

7. Take corrective action.

STEP 1: PLAN THE ASSESSMENT

The first task in planning the assessment is to select the assessment team and provide orientation in the assessment process for the team members. The team should be small—between two and five people. The assessment team typically includes individual contributors from the organization—for example, developers, improvement team members, and test engineers. The assessment team should not include any individuals who supervise the people being assessed. The interviewees should feel free to say what practices they are and are not implementing, without any fear of retribution from any assessment team member.

The next task in planning is to define the scope of the mini-assessment. The scope includes the project teams to be interviewed and the topics to be assessed (such as a life cycle phase or section of the improvement framework). When these have been selected, review the assessment questions with the assessment team and check that the questions are relevant to the people being interviewed.

STEP 2: MEET WITH THE INTERVIEWEES TO EXPLAIN WHAT WILL BE CHECKED AND HOW

Start with a short meeting (such as one hour) with all the participants and describe the mini-assessment process. Include the assessment team and members of the project teams you will be assessing. You can use the following agenda for this session:

- Objectives of the assessment (for example, to determine strengths and areas for improvement for each project assessed)
- Scope of the assessment (which projects will be assessed and on what topics)
- The members of the assessment team
- The mini-assessment interview session
- The data that will be communicated to the project and to the organization
- Sample results and debriefing

STEP 3: PERFORM THE MINI-ASSESSMENT INTERVIEW

The mini-assessment team interviews each project team during a group interview using the defined questions. Each interview session should not last more than two hours. After that time, the attention of the participants begins to dissipate. Two hours is adequate for approximately 40 to 60 questions with 6 to 10 interviewees in one session. Exceeding 10 people can make an interview unmanageable.

We recommend that you conduct a verbal interview to ensure the quality of the responses. For example, if the project team answered yes to the question, "Do you perform software configuration management of all critical work products?" you can ask clarifying questions about which critical work products are kept under control and how well the practice is working for the team. If the mini-assessment was a written survey with no interview component, extensive follow-up may be necessary to verify the results.

STEP 4: COMMUNICATE THE RESULTS

The first result of the mini-assessment is a summary of the strengths and areas for improvement for the project being assessed. During the mini-assessment process, the assessment team takes note of practices that are performed well and areas that need improvement. These notes are summarized and presented to the project at a follow-up communication session. An example is shown in Figure F–2.

The second result of the mini-assessment is the number of favorable responses from the mini-assessment questions. The assessment team calculates the percentage of favorable responses and communicates it back to each project. At the end of the communication session, the team members can select a few areas

---

Project A: Strengths and areas for improvement

Strengths

- Inspections are performed on requirements and code.
- Black-box testing is performed against the requirements.
- White-box testing is performed on critical code.
- Work products are under configuration management (in other words, project plans, requirements, code, test plans, and test cases).

Areas for improvement

- Computer network stability has not changed since it was reported in the last assessment.
- Project plans for projects larger than three months would benefit from inspection.
- Test plans would benefit from inspection to reduce the amount of redundancy in the test approach.

Figure F–2 A small example of mini-assessment results for one project.

for the next improvement phase and revise the improvement plan.

A bar chart indicating the overall percent of favorable responses graphically communicates the average project score for all projects assessed. The sample charts in Figures F–3 and F–4 show the trends of each group. If the organization is very large, you may decide to communicate the results separately for each major division.

In the example in Figure F–3, the organization performed mini-assessments every four months. The data indicates that during the first year, organization A made progress between January and May and lost ground in September. Attrition of personnel caused this decline. During the early stages of an improvement program, a few people drive the practices of the organization. If these people leave, the practices can leave too.

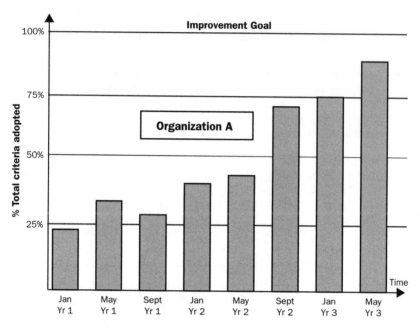

Figure F–3   Mini-assessment results over time.

In Figure F–4, another organization tabulated its mini-assessment data to show progress toward achieving CMM Level 2, broken down into 154 individual elements. They categorized responses to show partial satisfaction of the CMM components. Response categories were

- Not applicable

- None; little or no verbal or written evidence

- Weak; current practice or plans are weak or inadequate

- Some; project is approaching intent of key process area practice

- Strong; generally speaking, project fulfills CMM intent

The rough prediction line in Figure F–4 shows that all 154 elements might be complete by the second half of year 6 based

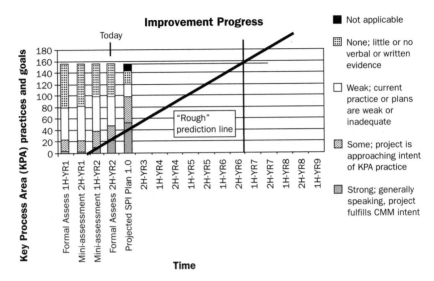

Figure F–4   Graph from mini-assessment data showing improvement progress (overall company average).

on actual progress since the first half of year 2. The action plan (see "Projected SPI Plan 1.0" in Figure F–4), developed for the first half of year 3, predicts that more elements will be adopted within the next six months. The rough prediction line is an early warning to the organization. Its precision is not important in this example. It is clear that the original target date for CMM Level 2, which was the first half of year 4, is impossible to meet.

When you track progress, we suggest you keep all individual project data in confidence. Each team can obtain data about its own progress for the purpose of its own improvement. The focus of management should be on organizationwide trends.

STEP 5: DEBRIEF THE MINI-ASSESSMENT PROCESS

A mini-assessment can cause resentment among the interviewees if it is not managed carefully. The interviewees may perceive it to be an audit, regardless of how well the mini-assessment is conducted. To make the process effective, the mini-assessment team needs to involve the organization before and after the mini-assessment. A debriefing with representatives of the projects assessed identifies the aspects of the mini-assessment process that were effective and the aspects that need to be improved. This debriefing typically takes two hours, using the following agenda:

- Brainstorm what the organization liked about the mini-assessment process

- Brainstorm areas for improvement of the mini-assessment process

- Combine or eliminate items as appropriate

- Set priorities to improve the mini-assessment process

- Create an action plan and assign responsibilities

STEP 6: IMPROVE THE QUESTIONNAIRE

In addition to debriefing the mini-assessment process, it is also beneficial to invite between three and ten interviewees to help revise the questions used during the mini-assessment. This review can help remove ambiguities in the questionnaire and elicit exam-

Table F–1   Questionnaire and Clarification of Question

Sample Mini-Assessment Questions	Explanation of the Practices
Perform inspections or walkthroughs for key work products (such as code, design, test cases, and test plans)?	To find defects systematically. The Gilb [Gilb93], Fagan [Fagan86], or Weinberg [Weinberg90] processes are acceptable.
Perform black-box testing?	The software is tested against the requirements specification and user guide.
Perform white-box testing?	Selected paths of the program's logic are systematically tested.

Sample Mini-Assessment Questions	Explanation of the Practices
Perform version control of all significant work products (from plans to code)?	Version control is conducted for all significant outputs created when using the standard development life cycle (for example, requirements, design, code, test cases, and user guide). Teams can use a tool or manual date-time stamps. At any time, team members know which versions of documents and code they are using and creating.
Have adequate computer network stability (compared with the problem reported in the last assessment)?	This was a key issue during the last assessment. It is a major problem if you lose more than four hours of network access per person per week.
Have adequate cross-site development version control (compared with the problem reported in the last assessment)?	This was an important issue during the last assessment. It is a major problem if you lose more than eight hours of productivity per person per week due to coordinating cross-site development and builds.
Agree to its commitments?	The team agrees that the deadlines and workload may be aggressive but are achievable.
Use a process for estimation?	A defined set of steps are executed to derive estimates. Examples include the use of a historical database, the Wideband Delphi estimation process, and the Constructive Cost Model [Boehm81].
Use a process for risk management?	A defined set of steps are executed to identify and manage risks.
Use a process for developing schedules?	A defined set of steps are executed to create a schedule that includes tasks, dependencies, estimates, resources, and high-risk mitigation actions.
Use a process for making commitments?	A defined set of steps are executed to determine, discuss, and agree on commitments between the project team, marketing, and the vice president.

ples to improve clarity. To facilitate improving the questionnaire, you can add a column to help describe the use or intent of the practices being advocated. Table F–1 shows an example.

STEP 7: TAKE CORRECTIVE ACTION

The results of the mini-assessment are a list of strengths and areas for improvement, and a score based on the number of practices adopted from the questionnaire. Three types of corrective action are typical following a mini-assessment:

1. Individual project teams revise their action plans.
2. The organization responds to an overall trend in the data.
3. Good practices are noted and shared across the organization.

Individual Project Teams Revise Their Action Plans

Corrective action is focused on addressing the areas for improvement noted in the assessment. Select a suitable time to address these findings based on the current goals and problems of the project team. For example, consider this item in Figure F–2: *Test plans would benefit from inspection to reduce the amount of redundancy in the test approach*. This improvement should be implemented when the project team creates its next test plan.

The Organization Responds to an Overall Trend in the Data

The data from several mini-assessments will indicate a trend in the organization's overall progress. Chapter 3 provides two examples describing companies that observed trends in their mini-assessment results. If your trend is down, consider the causes. Are people leaving the organization and taking skills with them, or is inadequate attention and time being spent on improvement? If the trend is up, is it enough to achieve any target you have set for framework adoption? Corrective actions include transitioning current best practices to other projects that have a need, spending more time on improvement, and using process champions to deploy best practices in parallel with the improvement team's efforts.

Think through your responses to trends in the data before taking action. For example, if the mini-assessment data shows that process-auditing activities are inadequate, consider which specific process audits would provide the most benefit. If the topic of requirements management is weak, determine specifically where in the project life cycle requirements management needs to be strengthened. Integrate corrective actions with current organizational goals and problems.

Good Practices Are Noted and Shared Across the Organization

Mini-assessments identify practices from which others can benefit. Share these by creating small workshops, using lunchtime discussion sessions, mentoring, creating newsletters, recording videos, presenting at division meetings, publishing examples of templates and processes, and posting summaries on a Web site. Don't rely solely on documentation for effective communication. Written processes make great reference material, but the material is not always read or understood.

References

[Basili84] Basili, V., and D. Weiss. "A Methodology for Collecting Valid Software Engineering Data." *IEEE Transactions on Software Engineering* 1984;SE-10(6):728–738.

[Block99] Block, P. *Flawless Consulting: A Guide to Getting Your Expertise Used*. 2nd ed. San Francisco: Jossey-Bass/Pfeiffer, 1999.

[Boehm81] Boehm, B. *Software Engineering Economics*. Englewood Cliffs, NJ: Prentice-Hall, 1981.

[Boehm89] Boehm, B. *Tutorial: Software Risk Management*. New York: IEEE Computer Society, 1989.

[Caputo98] Caputo, K. *CMM® Implementation Guide: Choreographing Software Process Improvement*. Reading, MA: Addison-Wesley, 1998.

[Carey67] Carey, A. "The Hawthorne Studies: A Radical Criticism." *American Sociological Review* 1967;32(3):403–416.

[Carr00] Carr, M., and N. Crowder. *Continuous Improvement Method (CAM): A New Paradigm for Benchmarking Process Maturity*. Presented at INCOSE 2000, Minneapolis, July 2000.

[Cassell92] Cassell, R. "Seven Steps to a Successful Customer Survey." *Quality Progress* July 1992.

[CMMI02] CMMI Product Development Team. *CMMI^{SM} for Systems Engineering/Software Engineering/Integrated Product and Process Development.* Version 1.1 (CMMI^{SM}-SE/ SW/IPPD, v1.1), staged representation. CMU/SEI-2002-TR-004, ESC-TR-2002-004, Pittsburgh: SEI, November 2002.

[Deming86] Deming, W. *Out of Crisis.* Cambridge: MIT Center for Advanced Engineering Study, 1986:88.

[Dion93] Dion, R. "Process Improvement and the Corporate Balance Sheet." *IEEE Software* 1993:10, no. 4:28–35.

[Dunaway96] Dunaway, D., and S. Masters. *CMM-Based Appraisal for Internal Process Improvement (CBA-IPI): Method Description.* (CMU/SEI-96-TR-007). Pittsburgh: Software Engineering Institute, Carnegie Mellon University, April 1996.

[Fagan86] Fagan, M. "Advances in Software Inspection." *IEEE Transactions on Software Engineering* SE-12(7):744–751.

[Florac99] Florac, W., and A. Carleton. *Measuring the Software Process: Statistical Process Control for Software Process Improvement.* Reading, MA: Addison-Wesley, 1999.

[Gilb93] Gilb, T., and D. Graham. *Software Inspection.* Essex, UK: Addison-Wesley, 1993.

[Grady87] Grady, R., and D. Caswell. *Software Metrics: Establishing a Company-wide Program.* Englewood Cliffs, NJ: Prentice-Hall, 1987.

[Grady92] Grady, R. *Practical Software Metrics for Project Management and Process Improvement.* Englewood Cliffs, NJ: Prentice-Hall, 1992.

[Grady97] Grady, R. *Successful Software Process Improvement.* Englewood Cliffs, NJ: Prentice Hall, 1997.

[Hill79] Hill, N. *Law of Success.* Northbrook, IL: Success Unlimited, 1979:1–67.

[Humphrey89] Humphrey, W. "Software Quality Assurance." In: *Managing the Software Process.* Reading, MA: Addison-Wesley, 1989:137–153.

[Humphrey95] Humphrey, W. *A Discipline for Software Engineering.* Reading, MA: Addison-Wesley, 1995.

[Jalote00] Jalote, P. *CMM in Practice: Processes for Executing Software Projects at Infosys.* Boston: Addison-Wesley, 2000: 291–304.

[Moore91] Moore, G. *Crossing the Chasm.* New York: Harper-Business, 1991.

[Paulk93] Carnegie Mellon University/Software Engineering Institute. Edited by: M. Paulk, C. Weber, B. Curtis and M. B. Chrissis. *The Capability Maturity Model: Guidelines for Improving the Software Process.* Reading, MA: Addison-Wesley, 1995.

[Peters85] Peters, T., and N. Austin. *A Passion for Excellence.* New York: Warner Books, 1985:356.

[Potter01] Potter, N., and M. Sakry. "Keep Your Project on Track." *Software Development* 2001; 9, no. 4.

[Robbins98] Robbins A. *The Time of Your Life.* Audiocassette program. San Diego: Robbins Research International, 1998.

[Rogers62] Rogers, E. *Diffusion of Innovations.* New York: The Free Press, 1962.

[Sakry01] Potter, N., and M. Sakry. "Practical CMM." *Software Development* 2001;9:65–69.

[Sakry93] Potter, N., and M. Sakry. *Software Engineering Process Group Workshop.* Dallas: The Process Group, 1993.

[SCAMPI00] CMMI Project Development Team. *SCAMPI, V1.0, Standard CMMI Assessment Method for Process Improvement: Method Description.* Version 1.0, CMU/SEI-2000-TR-009. Pittsburgh: SEI, 2000.

[Van Scoy92] Van Scoy, Roger L. *Software Development Risk: Opportunity, Not Problem.* CMU/SEI-92-TR-30, ADA 258743. Pittsburgh: SEI, 1992.

[Weinberg85] Weinberg, G. *The Secrets of Consulting: A Guide to Giving and Getting Advice Successfully.* New York: Dorset House Publishing, 1985.

[Weinberg97] Weinberg, G. *Quality Software Management. Vol. 4, Anticipating Change.* New York: Dorset House Publishing, 1997.

[Weinberg90] Weinberg, G., and D. Freedman. *Handbook of Walkthroughs, Inspections, and Technical Reviews.* 3rd ed. New York: Dorset House Publishing, 1990.

[Westfall99] Westfall, L. "Customer Satisfaction." *Software Testing and Quality Engineering* 1999;1(4):52–59.

[Wiegers99] Wiegers, K. *Software Requirements*. Redmond, WA: Microsoft Press, 1999.

[Yamamura97] Yamamura, G., and G. Wigle. "SEI CMM Level 5: For the Right Reasons." *CROSSTALK—The Journal of Defense Software Engineering*. 1997;10,8:3–8.

[Zahran98] Zahran, S. *Software Process Improvement—Practical Guidelines for Business Success*. Essex, UK: Addison-Wesley, 1998.

Index

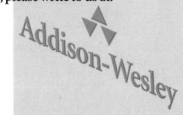